BattlePages

Tales of Numera

THE PRISONER

Matt Walker

Combined Adventure Story + Educational Study Book
Year 5 Maths Part 1

First published in Great Britain in 2021 by Matt Walker

www.walkerproductions.co.uk

Twitter: @_mattwalker
Facebook Page: @mattwalkerproductions
Instagram: walkerproductions.co.uk

Also by Matt Walker:

SHEET MUSIC TITLES
Essential Black Composers For The Advanced Pianist
EP.IC: Bach
EP.IC: Beethoven
Lesson One To Grade One
Fairies & Unicorns (Piano Fantasy)
Hansel & Gretel (Piano Poems)
65 Easy Classics For Electronic Keyboard (Just Three Chords!)
Favourite Children's Songs For Piano Duet
65 Easy Songs For Electronic Keyboard (Just Three Chords!)
Step-By-Step Sight Reading For Piano
Six New Choral Pieces For Youth & Children's Choirs
110 Easy Pieces For Piano; The Ultimate Bumper Collection
Favourite Children's Songs For Piano
More Favourite Children's Songs For Piano (with Annabel Walker)
Favourite Children's Songs For Piano… & More!
Favourite Children's Classics For Piano (Book 1)
Favourite Children's Christmas For Piano
Light & Shade (assorted compositions)
American Folk Songs: Favorite Melodies For Really Easy Piano
Nursery Rhymes: Favourite Melodies For Really Easy Piano
Christmas Favourites: Favourite Melodies For Really Easy Piano
Favourite Melodies For Really Easy Piano: The Complete Collection

MAGIC BOOK TITLES
How To Do Magic: Professional Effects For Beginners
Mercury: A Book Test (under the pseudonym LM Wood)

NOVELS
The Beyond | Shark Bait | Memories Unspeakable

Introduction

Welcome. You made it. This cold, wet, God-forsaken hole in the middle of the mountains. Dark. Dank. It's hard to breathe down here. You haven't seen the sun in a long, long time.

This old gold mine is your home, and has been for nearly a year.

In this world, you are not yourself. You couldn't be. You are on the planet Numera, which is like our own in a lot of ways, but very different in others.

Your name is 369. At least, that's what they call you. When they learn your true name they will regret the day they made you a prisoner.

This book uses my *BattlePage* battle system. The enemies you will face get stronger as the story unfolds. You need to get stronger too, and to do that you need to complete the practise exercises and timed tests. The harder you work the stronger you'll get.

You may find it useful to have an adult to help you every now and then, but it's not necessary.

Look at the character card below. This is you.

Ragged. Filthy. You don't look like much, do you? But just wait.

	Strength	*Full:*	
	Speed	*Full:*	
	Will	*Full:*	
	Reputation		
	Items:		

Spells:	ARROW RAIN	~	Cost: **6 will**	Damage 6 to **all** enemies in battle
	VORTEX	~	Cost: **8 will**	Damage 12 to **one** enemy

There are a few attributes to understand. Your **Strength** score tells you how strong you are. The stronger you are the more powerful your attacks, and the more damage you can take. You lose strength points during battle, when you get hit. You can regain these strength points and return to *full strength* with a little rest, recuperation, a bit of first aid, or maybe even a bit of healing magic. Your *full strength* has its own little bubble on the character card. It is slightly shaded in. You can increase your full strength score by completing the exercises and timed tests. The more you practise your maths, the better you'll get, and the *stronger* you'll get.

Your **Speed** score is all about your agility, movement, and reflexes. The faster you are, the more likely you'll be to get in that first hit. If you have good reflexes, you're more likely to block an enemy's attack — perhaps they'll only strike you a glancing blow, minimising the damage. Or maybe you'll dodge it all together. The faster you are, the less damage an enemy can do to you. Be careful though — wearing heavy armour, or carrying heavy weapons, lowers your speed.

Then there's your **Will**. This score is all about your strength of mind. There are certain... *abilities* (of which you will discover more later) requiring a lot of concentration — a lot of *will*. These abilities will be very important to your journey.

Lastly, you have your **Reputation**. Your choices throughout the story will affect your reputation, and how other characters interact with you, friend or foe. You can get a bad reputation by making bad choices.

What I want you to do now is cut out your rectangular character cards on the opposite page with some scissors. There are four of them — but they're double-sided, so you actually have eight. You will use these in your battles, writing down your **strength**, **speed**, **will**, and **reputation** scores, and any items you collect. You can use your current character card as a bookmark. Keep the spares somewhere safe. If you need more, you can print them off from my website - www.walkerproductions.co.uk

Also, if you like this book, please do leave a review on Amazon! As a small publisher, reviews are really important to us.

You

The *BattlePage* battle system is pretty simple. When you attack an enemy, the enemy sustains *damage*. The damage they take is calculated by this simple formula:

Your strength **take away** their speed = the damage they take.

So if your strength is 10 and their speed is 5, the damage they take is 10-5 = 5.
   You then take the damage off their strength.

When an enemy attacks you, the same formula applies, but it's *their* strength take away *your* speed.
   You'll learn how my *BattlePage* battle system works in more detail a bit later. But for now, it's time for you to join the story.

This world, Numera, has been waiting for you.

CHAPTER ONE:
The Choosing

Digging.

The sound of metal striking stone. It echoes through the mine shaft. Sometimes it's so hot down here it's suffocating. Sometimes it's so cold your dishevelled rags barely stop your shivers. You don't know why some of the mine shafts are colder than others, though it probably has something to do with the underground river rushing through the caves deep beneath you still.

There used to be hundreds of prisoners like you, it seemed. The cells were packed to bursting. You could barely move. People had to sleep sitting up, because there wasn't enough floor space for everyone to lie down.

There is now.

There are only thirteen in your cell at the moment — a cell that had once held fifty. The others have been taken away. You don't know where, exactly. Only that it's called The Pit. And when people are taken to work there they never come back.

You don't know what they're doing down there. No one does.

One of the guards shows up at your cell. He raps the bars with the hilt of his sword. Makes them sing. Those sleeping startle awake. "Get up," he says.

You know what's coming. It's been happening every week for the last few months. And your stomach knots, because there are far less of you now. Far less for the master to choose from.

Every time it gets more and more likely he'll pick you.

The guard leaves your cell and heads to the next.

"I got a feeling it's me this time." Five Twelve has appeared at your shoulder. He looks older than he is. Working in a gold mine will do that to a person. "I think my luck has run out."

"It ran out when you got bought by Al'Nor," you say, and he laughs.

Ain't that the truth.

You listen to the guards rousing the rest of the prisoners, and hear the main gate clank open and a phalanx of knights march in. *Here we go again.* Then you see them. They march to the front of the room and turn to face you all. In the middle stands Al'Nor, the master of this gold mine.

He is an old man, but somehow over the last few months he seems to have got *younger*. His hair is still grey, and his skin is still like old leather, but he is more sprightly, as if The Pit (whatever that is) has given him a new lease of life.

Towering over him is his High Protector, Caesar, who looks around the room with his lip curled and one hand on the sword at his hip. There are four other bodyguards flanking Al'Nor, all wearing red surcoats over their armour. The other knights wear blue.

"Open the cells," Al'Nor says.

The guards turn cranks and the cell doors slide open one-by-one. The knights shift positions, hands on hilts, just in case a mutiny is about to occur. But you prisoners have no weapons, no energy, and no resistance.

There was a time when the guards would only open one cell at a time, but with so few of you they have little reason to worry.

Al'Nor sighs. "Look at them." He spits on the floor. "Pitiful. Most are either old, or weak." He points to an elderly lady. "What are we supposed to do with her? We need more prisoners. Young and strong. Useful." He looks pointedly at Caesar, who nods.

"We've bought out all the town prisons for miles around, Sir."

"Look harder. Look *further*. I don't care. We need more." Then he says under his breath, "I don't care *how* you get them, just *get* them, okay?" Then he growls and waves a hand. "Call them. Hurry up. They need to start work."

Caesar unfurls a roll of parchment. "If you hear your number, come out of your cell and make a line in front of me."

Five Twelve whispers, "If I get picked... thank you for being my friend."

Worksheet Topic 1
BIG NUMBERS

It is time to complete your first maths worksheet. Not only will this advance the story, it will also improve your attributes (your strength, speed and will). Exciting, right? You can write in pencil in this book, or on a scrap bit of paper. You will find all the answers on page 12.

After you've completed the exercises, mark it, fill in your attributes, and then carry on with the story.

Caesar stands before you with the unrolled parchment between his hands. You prisoners each have a number. Yours is 369. Your best friend is 512. Some prisoners have much higher numbers than you.

Numbers have *place value*. The number **7 523 274** is a very big number. In the *millions*. You can partition big numbers into groups of three, starting from the right (the smallest number), to make them easier to read. Sometimes, these groups of three are separated with commas instead of spaces: **7,523,274**.

Let's put this big number into a place value table.

Millions	Hundred Thousands	Ten Thousands	Thousands	Hundreds	Tens	Ones
7	5	2	3	2	7	4

So this massive number (so big it doesn't even fit on one line) is:
7 million, five hundred and twenty-three thousand, two hundred and seventy-four.

Notice that the written-out number is *also* partitioned into groups of three, starting from the right (the *smallest number*), by commas.

Exercises

1] Write the following big numbers into the place value table below.
Tip: For each question, start with the smallest number (the <u>Ones</u>, which are furthest on the right).

a) 5 128 467   b) 186 290   c) 3 836 572

d) 8 389   e) 25 121

	Millions	Hundred Thousands	Ten Thousands	Thousands	Hundreds	Tens	Ones
A	5	1	2	8	4	6	7
B		1	8	6	2	9	0
C	3	8	3	6	5	7	2
D				8	3	8	9
E			2	5	1	2	1

Now double check you've filled it in correctly by comparing it to the answer table at the top of page 12. All good? Okay, answer the questions on page 11.

2] Write out those five numbers in words. The first has been done for you.

a) *Five million, one hundred and twenty-eight thousand, four hundred and sixty-seven*

b) One hundred and eight, six thousand, two hundred and nighty

c) Three million, eight hundred and thirty-six thousand, five hundred and seventy-two

d) eight thousand, three hundred and eighty nine

e) twenty five thousand, one hundred and twenty one.

3] Now, using your filled-in table to help, put those numbers in ascending order (that means smallest to largest). I've written them out again below.

| 5 128 467, | 186 290, | 3 836 572, | 8 389, | 25 121 |

8,389, 25, 121, 186, 290, 3,836,572, 5,128,467 ✓

4] Put these numbers in ascending order. You may want to draw another place value table on a scrap piece of paper and fill them in first.

| 62 231, | 7 100 263, | 2 703, | 1 023 904, | 245 004 |

2,703, 62,231, 245,004, 1,023,904, 7,100,263 ✓

5] Now write out your number (369) and your best friend's number (512) in words. *For example, '123' would be written 'one hundred and twenty-three'.*

369: three hundred and sixty-nine ✓

512: five hundred and twelve ✓

Now check and mark your answers using page 12. How did you do? Don't worry if you made a mistake. Try and see where you went wrong. Now take your current character card and pick up a pencil. Fill it in like this:

Full strength: 4   **Full speed: 2**   **Full will: 0**   **Reputation: 4**

Go to page 13.

1]

	Millions	Hundred Thousands	Ten Thousands	Thousands	Hundreds	Tens	Ones
A	5	1	2	8	4	6	7
B		1	8	6	2	9	0
C	3	8	3	6	5	7	2
D				8	3	8	9
E			2	5	1	2	1

2]

a) *Five million, one hundred and twenty-eight thousand, four hundred and sixty-seven*

b) *One hundred and eighty-six thousand, two hundred and ninety*

c) *Three million, eight hundred and thirty-six thousand, five hundred and seventy-two*

d) *Eight thousand, three hundred and eighty-nine*

e) *Twenty-five thousand, one hundred and twenty-one*

3] 8 389,   25 121,   186 290,   3 836 572,   5 128 467

4] 2 703,   62 231,   245 004,   1 023 904,   7 100 263

5] **369:** *Three hundred and sixty-nine*

    512: *Five hundred and twelve*

Caesar goes through his list, calling numbers, calling names.

Prisoners' shoulders slump as they hear their own.

They move out of their cells and make a line in front of the High Protector.

Nine of them. Ten. Eleven.

And then Caesar calls, "Five Hundred And Twelve."

You see Five Twelve next to you drop his head. "I told you," he whispers.

You swallow. "I'm sorry, my friend."

"And lastly," Caesar adds, "Three Hundred and Sixty-Nine."

Five Twelve stops, and looks back.

That's you.

CHAPTER TWO:
My Name Is

You follow Five Twelve out of the cell.

Well, you've always wondered what's down The Pit. Guess now you're going to find out.

As you join the line Al'Nor looks you up and down, and then his gaze lingers on your eyes, and for a moment you wonder if he knows who you really are... but then he looks past you at the next prisoner.

If you only knew, you think. *If I only had some water...*

The measly cup they give you to drink each day is enough to sustain you, but nothing more. If you had a bucket, however... If they let you wash in something more than a dirty puddle every month...

Al'Nor is going down the line himself now, inspecting the prisoners chosen out for him. Caesar follows close by, should anyone try anything.

He stops in front of a thin, wiry man, and prods his belly. "This one won't do. Look at him. He's skin and bone."

"His captain speaks highly of him, Sir, else we wouldn't have chosen him."

Al'Nor pulls a face. "Well okay." He moves on to the next, and the next, and then suddenly he's standing in front of you again.

He looks at you for a long time without saying a word. Then he speaks. "Where are you from?"

"Southern Sha'Pan," you lie.

"How old are you?"

"I can't remember, Sir."

"How long have you been here?"

"Nearly a year."

Al'Nor doesn't take his eyes off you, but he says to Caesar, "Tell me where we found this one."

"Errr..." Caesar pulls out a small, battered notebook from his waistbag and flicks through the pages. "Let me see... yes, Three Hundred And Sixty-Nine – it says we paid a trader direct. Didn't cost much."

"We bought you off a trader." Al'Nor squints into your face. "Tell me... where did the trader find you?"

In the middle of the mountains. Broken and beaten. Half-dead with the fall, and the fire. Lucky to be alive, after what I'd been fighting.

You say, "I was travelling across Sha'Pan. Alone. He robbed me and sold me to you."

"A highwayman, you say."

You shrug. "It was more of a dirt track than a highway."

Al'Nor starts laughing. Then he turns to Caesar. "Take them to The Pit."

The guards crank shut the cells, and the phalanx of knights and bodyguards escort Al'Nor back out of the room. Caesar stays behind until they have left, then he walks up and down the line himself.

"You have been chosen," he says, "because we know you will work hard. Am I correct?"

You all murmur about how correct he is.

"Good. Captain! Take them."

The captain is a brute with a helmet and leather armour, and a plaited ponytail that hangs down his back. He strides up to you all and roars something, though it sounds like gibberish. He carries a mace, which is basically a club with spikes on it, and he waves it around like a caveman.

Then he leads the lot of you (there are thirteen including yourself, you've counted) across the room and out through the gate opposite the one Al'Nor just left by. You have been through this gate every day since you got here.

The corridor branches into three. To your left is the rock-hewn staircase leading down and down to the mine shaft you prisoners call *the freezer*. It's cold, if you haven't guessed from the name.

It is not your favourite place to work.

To your right is another descending staircase leading to an equally cold little cavern called *the ice box*, which hasn't been mined for a good while, because the gold has all been dug out.

The central corridor winds up and up, and that's where you're led. Five Twelve says, "At least we'll be warm."

Five guards join their captain, these carrying clubs.

There are more mine shafts on different levels, most abandoned now. Captain Plaited Ponytail takes you into one of the disused ones, which for some reason is lit with wall torches.

Five Twelve whispers to you, "They used to call this one *the oven*, I'm sure, because of how hot it got."

"I thought they'd stopped digging here."

"They have."

"*Quiet!*" Captain Ponytail smacks his mace against the wall, making it ring.

You fall silent, lest the next smack be against your head.

The shaft takes a bend and then rises, and you take a breath – all you prisoners do – because it looks like... no, you're sure it *is*... it's *daylight*. Daylight at the end of the tunnel, and you haven't seen daylight for so long (you can't even tell when night falls, down in the cells).

"Oh my God..." says Five Twelve.

Prisoners start laughing, and whooping and cheering.

I don't care what The Pit has in store for me, you think. *It'll be worth it, just to see the sun one last time.*

"Settle down, settle down," says Captain Ponytail.

You're all moving quicker now. The patch of light is growing. It's so blurry and fuzzy because your eyes aren't used to it, but everything slowly comes into focus.

You're in throwing distance of the end of the tunnel when someone at the front of the line shouts, "It's raining!"

And his words stop you dead.

Raining.

Could it be true?

Unfortunately, the clubman behind walks straight into you.

"Hey, slug! *Get moving.*"

Then he thrashes you with his club.

This is him. Scarred. Lank hair. Thick, scraggy beard. You wouldn't want him dating your mother, would you.

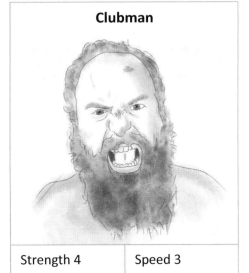

Clubman

| Strength 4 | Speed 3 |

Here's a really basic introduction into how my *BattlePage Battle System* works. You'll be pleased to know, you're normally the faster and get to attack first. But this clubman has hit you from behind, and you barely knew anything about it. This is called a *sneak attack*. Getting smacked with his club hurts.

Go get your character card.

Now look at the clubman's strength score above. It's **4**.

You get damaged by his **strength** score (4) **minus** your **speed**. Your speed is 2.

You get damaged by: 4-2 = 2.

So you need to knock 2 points off your strength score. Your full strength is 4. Take 2 away from 4 and you get 2. So write a *2* in your strength box, next to the full strength bubble.

The blow sends you staggering against the wall. You let out a low *oof*. Five Twelve pulls you to your feet and helps you get moving again.

Your side kills. You think maybe the thug broke a rib or two. But you'll show him. And how.

As you get closer, you realise there's a gate blocking the way. The daylight pours through the iron bars. There's another guard at the gate, and he nods at Captain Ponytail and winches it open.

The prisoners make it out into the daylight, into the sunshine, into the rain. You're at the bottom of a huge canyon, high rock walls towering around you, the ground underfoot dark and wet.

The others slow their walk, laughing and cheering up into the sky, inclining their heads and opening their mouths.

You don't join in the laughter, or the dancing. And when Five Twelve gives you a clap on the back and yells, "I can see the sun! Ow, my eyes!" you don't reply.

You just stand, statuesque, feeling the rain soak into your skin.

And by God there's power in that water.

Because there's magic in *you* - water magic - and you feel it stirring inside, growing strong. Magic you haven't felt for nearly a year is coursing through your veins again. Your muscles clench, and your hands clench, and you lift your head to the sky and breathe it all in.

"Alright, alright!" yells the captain. "You've felt the rain on your skin, now get moving!" He gestures to the other end of the canyon. Far across the boulder field is a makeshift wooden wall. You can't pick out much detail from this distance, but you know there must be guards patrolling it, and you know The Pit must lie beyond.

And you know that if you walk in you won't be walking out again.

You stare at Captain Ponytail, and at the other guards walking up and down the line.

Five Twelve nudges you. "Hey? Come on. *Hey.*" He nudges you harder. "What are you doing? Don't stare at them, you'll get beat again..."

"Do you know something?" you say. "Over the past year you've become my friend, and yet I don't even know your real name."

Five Twelve swallows. "I... I'm... we don't *have* real names now."

You look at him. "Yes we do."

"We..."

"My name is Aquaan." It feels good to say it, after all this time. "And I am an Elemental."

CHAPTER THREE:
Daylight And Rain

You are one of the Eleven.

Elemental mages with extraordinary powers.

Unknown across all Numera until the event known as The Rising. Even now many people doubt your existence. Although everyone has heard of the Eleven.

You are here because Numera is under threat, along with all living things on this world. For nearly a year you've been held prisoner, unable to use your powers.

Until now.

It's like electricity, your magic flooding back. To activate it, you need to complete this short test on the two and ten times tables. First, make sure you've memorised the times tables shown below. Hopefully you know them pretty well already. They're the easy ones.

The Two Times Table					
1x2=2	2x2=4	3x2=6	4x2=8	5x2=10	6x2=12
7x2=14	8x2=16	9x2=18	10x2=20	11x2=22	12x2=24

The Ten Times Table					
1x10=10	2x10=20	3x10=30	4x10=40	5x10=50	6x10=60
7x10=70	8x10=80	9x10=90	10x10=100	11x10=110	12x10=120

Before you start, I want you to cover the answers, which are at the top of the next page. Do it now. Use some paper, a book, your cat – anything. Okay? Done? Now get a scrap piece of paper to write the answers on. **Don't write them in this book**, because you may have to retake the test. You also need a stopwatch or a timer. Get an adult to help you, if you need to. You have **90 seconds** to complete the test. You need to get at least 16 correct to activate your magic. If you don't quite make it, revise the times tables above and retake the test.

THE TEST				
1)5x2= 10	2)9x10= 90	3)2x2= 4	4)7x10=70	5)10x2=20
6)3x10= 30	7)12x2= 24	8)11x10=110	9)6x2= 12	10)5x10=50
11)1x2= 2	12)8x10= 80	13)11x2=22	14)4x10= 40	15)4x2=8
16)10x10=100	17)2x2= 40	18)6x10= 60	19)12x10=120	20)9x2=18

Power pulses through you. You feel your broken ribs mend themselves. The scars criss-crossing your hands and arms fade.

You can make changes to your character card. Rub it out and fill it in like this:

Full strength: 8 **Full speed:** 5 **Full will:** 6 **Reputation:** 15

That looks better, doesn't it?

Five Twelve hasn't replied to your revelation. But he believes you. You can tell.

"Stay back," you tell him. "I don't want you getting killed because of me."

It looks like he tries to say something, but his mouth won't work.

"*You are really asking for it...*" It's the guard who hit you before. You turn to look at him. He is striding over, raising his club.

You're not going to let him hit you a second time. Your speed is 5. It's more than his strength, which is 4. This means he can do you no damage.

Clubman

Strength ~~4~~ 0	Speed 3

He swings his club at you, and you catch it, tear it out of his hands and toss it into the dirt. He is shocked still.

Now your turn to attack him.

Your strength is 8. His speed is 3.

Your strength (8) minus his speed (3) = 5, so he gets damaged by 5.

His strength is only 4, so he gets defeated with one hit. You send him sailing across the canyon, and he doesn't get back up again.

"*I said 'stay back*,'" you growl at Five Twelve, shoving him away as another clubman runs at you. You kick the guard's legs out from under him before he can even take a swing.

Then you hear the crunch of boots on sand behind you, almost lost under the thundering rain, and when you turn round there's the guard captain swinging his spiked mace.

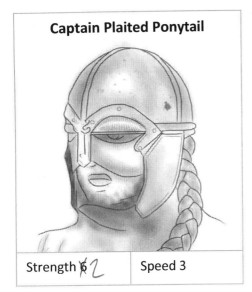

Captain Plaited Ponytail

Strength 6 2   Speed 3

This is a <u>sneak attack</u>, meaning you didn't see your enemy coming, so he gets in the first attack. Captain Ponytail's strength is **6**. His speed is **3**.

He sneak attacks you. The damage you sustain is 6 (his strength) – 5 (your speed) = 1. Go ahead and subtract 1 from your strength score, writing **7** in your character strength box, next to the *full strength* bubble. You do not need to cross out the 8 in the *full strength* bubble.

So you manage to dodge the worst of the spikes, but get struck a glancing blow. No worries – tis but a scratch.

It's now your turn to attack Captain Ponytail.

Notice that your strength is now *7*, NOT 8. When you get hurt, injured and tired, your attacks do less damage.

7 (your strength) – 3 (his speed) is 4, so he gets damaged by 4. Subtract 4 from his strength. Cross out the 6 and write *2* on his character card, in his strength box.

You've managed to knock him to his knees, and I assume his helmet's come flying off and you can see it now, rolling across the sand dunes.

It's Captain Ponytail's turn. He ain't looking too great. His strength is only 2 and your speed is 5, so when he wildly swings his mace at you a second time you dodge it easily. No damage done to you. Your strength stays at 7.

Your turn. I have a feeling this may be it, don't you? Your strength (7) – his speed (3) is 4, so he gets damaged by 4, which is more than enough to finish him off.

Captain Ponytail falls at your feet. Five Twelve just stands there dumbly with his mouth open, as do the other prisoners, as if they're playing a game of musical statues and the music's stopped.

The three remaining clubmen guards ignore them and run at you.

You haven't had time to heal yet, so your attributes are the same as before: strength 7, speed 5. But you still have 8 written in your *full strength* bubble. It's important that you do not lose your current character card with this information. Use it as a bookmark, okay?

You can see the brutes you're facing at the top of the next page.

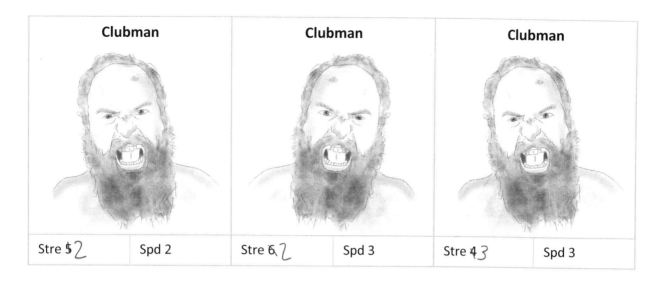

Clubman	Clubman	Clubman
Stre $5~2$ Spd 2	Stre $6~2$ Spd 3	Stre $4~3$ Spd 3

You are faster than all of them, so you can attack first, and you get to choose *who* to attack. Now, think about your tactics. Only one of these clubmen could do you some damage. Which one?

Yes. The middle one, with strength 6. The other two only have strength 5 and 4, and because your speed is 5 they can do you no damage.

The middle guy can do you 1 damage, because his strength (6) – your speed (5) = 1. <u>So you should hit him first.</u>

Do so now.

Your strength (7) – his speed (3) = 4. So subtract 4 damage from his strength. This leaves him with just 2 strength points remaining, and he ain't gonna be able to do much with that, bless him. Write **2** in his strength box and cross out the 6.

Okay, that's your turn done. You won't be able to attack anyone again until all 3 of your enemies have had their go.

The enemies take their turns from left to right.

So the one on the left attacks you first, but your speed matches his strength, so he can't hurt you. Then the middle one who's nearly dead – he tries to swing his club but barely has the strength to lift it, and he probably falls over. Lastly, the guy on the right can't hit you either.

Do you see now why we hit the guy in the middle first? If you'd attacked one of the others you'd have killed them with one punch. Fine. But the middle guy would have done *you* damage straight after. Just 1 point from your strength, but every point counts.

It's your turn again, and I reckon you can finish the battle yourself. Choose one to attack. You defeat them. The other two can't hurt you, so defeat the next one, and then there's just one guy remaining, and he's no match for you either.

You getting the hang of thc battle system now? Good.

CHAPTER FOUR:
Magic

The guards lie in the dust and the rain. Before you have a chance to say anything a long howl echoes over the canyon.

"Mountain wolves…" says one of the prisoners, the tallest in your group.

You all look to the cliff tops. The wolves' dark silhouettes are visible against the sky.

"T-they won't be interested in us?" asks another. "Will they?"

"The blood has drawn them. They can smell it for miles."

"Agh, yer just kickin up a fuss, Twenty-Three. They ain't gonna hurt us."

"I've lived in these mountains all my life," growls the tall one, whose name is apparently Twenty-Three. *Don't you think I know a bit more about mountain wolves than you?*" He looks back at the mine. "We need to go. Now."

"Where?" says Five Twelve. "They shut the gate behind us. We can't go back."

"The wolves ain't gonna bother with us. Keep yer knickers on."

That's when the mountain wolves start scaling the cliffs. Jumping from craggy outcrop to sheer ledge to rocky slope. Down they come. Six of them, you count.

"Oh damn."

The prisoners look like they're going to scatter until you hold up a hand. "Wait. I've got this."

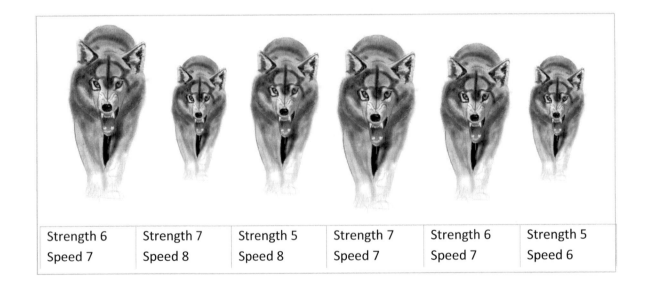

Strength 6	Strength 7	Strength 5	Strength 7	Strength 6	Strength 5
Speed 7	Speed 8	Speed 8	Speed 7	Speed 7	Speed 6

You can see from the wolves' faces that these doggies are fast and strong and savage. In fact, if you try engaging them in hand-to-hand combat I'm afraid things don't look good for you.

Luckily you have your magic to help you. Look at the *SPELLS* on your character card. You can't perform **VORTEX** yet – you don't have enough **will** – but you *can* perform **ARROW RAIN**. It costs *6 will* points and does *6 damage* 'to all enemies in battle' regardless of their speed. Your spells require a water source, which you have (it's raining). And as long as your enemy hasn't sneak attacked, you can cast a spell at the start of battle.

You cannot cast a spell mid-battle.

Not yet, anyway. You can only cast at the very start.

BUT. You must activate your magic by completing a maths test. You have **90 seconds** and must get 16 or more to be able to use *Arrow Rain* on the wolves.

First make sure you know your three and four times tables. Say the equations over and over again, until they're firmly in your head, like your favourite song lyrics.

The Three Times Table

1x3=3	2x3=6	3x3=9	4x3=12	5x3=15	6x3=18
7x3=21	8x3=24	9x3=27	10x3=30	11x3=33	12x3=36

The Four Times Table

1x4=4	2x4=8	3x4=12	4x4=16	5x4=20	6x4=24
7x4=28	8x4=32	9x4=36	10x4=40	11x4=44	12x4=48

Now take the test, writing the answers on a scrap piece of paper. Use a stopwatch or timer, just like last time.

THE TEST

1)5x3= 15	2)9x3= 27	3)2x3= 6	4)7x3= 21	5)8x3= 24
6)3x3= 9	7)12x3= 36	8)11x3= 33	9)6x3= 18	10)4x3= 12
11)1x4= 4	12)8x4= 32	13)3x4= 12	14)12x4= 48	15)4x4= 16
16)10x4= 40	17)2x4= 8	18)6x4= 24	19)9x4= 36	20)12x4= 48

Turn over to find the answers on page 24 and mark it. If you got 16 or more, you're in business. Let's turn that rain to arrows and feather those pups. If you fell short, don't worry. Simply do some more revision and retake the test.

ANSWERS

1) 15	2) 27	3) 6	4) 21	5) 24	6) 9	7) 36
8) 33	9) 18	10) 12	11) 4	12) 32	13) 12	14) 48
15) 16	16) 40	17) 8	18) 24	19) 36	20) 48	

So, the wolves are bearing down on you. No problem. You're an Elemental after all. Arrow Rain costs 6 will points, so subtract 6 from your will, writing **0** in the box next to your 'full will' bubble (which has a 6 in it). The spell is cast.

You hold your hands aloft and bend the thundering rain to your will. The water droplets merge into shear arrow head points, a thousand of them glistening overhead. And then by thrashing your arms down the Arrow Rain lashes into the approaching wolf pack.

The spell does 6 damage to all enemies in battle, meaning every wolf gets hit for 6, *regardless of their speed*. All but two of the wolfies die straight away. The two remaining survive with just 1 strength point left.

These survivors let out high-pitched shrieks.

And that's when the cliffs start to crumble.

Boulders crash down as the canyon's side gives way, like a brown and yellow waterfall, almost liquid in appearance. The wolves disappear in the landslide.

Rock crashes to the canyon floor, mere metres away from you all.

And then it goes *through* it.

The mine shaft running below collapses under the weight and the impact. The ground opens up like a yawning mouth.

You and the other prisoners let out yells of surprise, leaping back from the widening hole.

Five Twelve is not so lucky.

You see the ground dropping out from beneath his feet. And then you notice the body of the guard captain slide into the collapsing shaft. And you notice his mace. You've had your eye on that weapon for a while. No doubt it'll improve your strength. But the mace is now slipping into the hole. So is Five Twelve.

You can only save one of them - the mace or Five Twelve.

What do you do?

○ To save the mace and leave Five Twelve to his doom, **go to page 26.**

○ To save Five Twelve and let the mace fall, **go to page 25.**

Of course, it is no choice. Five Twelve has become something like a brother to you.

You dive forward and manage to grab his wrist as the ground disappears from beneath his feet.

The ground shifts slightly beneath you, too, and for one horrible moment you think you're both going to tumble to your deaths. But then it settles, supporting your weight, just about.

You haul Five Twelve up over the lip of the collapsed shaft as dust plumes up around you, as rock and sand and debris crash down far below.

Other prisoners join you, and together you drag the man to safety.

You clap him on the back and climb to your feet.

The other prisoners are breathing heavily, staring at you. They gather in an arc with Five Twelve on one end. The rain has washed the dirt and grime and sand off all of them, and you.

Not one of them speaks.

"Gather the water skins," you say. "Drink, all of you. Then fill them up with the rain, as full as you can."

They do so, no question.

Five Twelve brings you a water skin. "Do you even need this?"

"What do you mean?"

"Do you even need to drink?"

You laugh. "Yes. Thanks." You take it, a series of long, thirsty gulps.

He says, "Thanks for saving me."

And you shrug. "Don't worry about it."

"I'm Gord," says Five Twelve. "My name. My real name. Is Gord."

"Gourd? Like the vegetable?"

"I guess. But spelled differently. So they say. Not that I can write."

You nod. "Gord. I like it."

"Better than Five Twelve, anyway."

"At least your number rolled off the tongue."

He laughs. "So. What's the plan?"

For saving Five Twelve's life, your reputation goes up by 2. Go ahead and adjust it to 17 on your character card now.

Go to page 28.

It's a dog eat dog world, right? Out here in the mountains of Sha'Pan it's every man for himself.

You dive across the ground and grab the spiked mace just before it rolls into the abyss.

Then you turn to Five Twelve, to offer your hand, but it's too late.

The ground disappears beneath his feet, and he screams as he falls, and is swallowed by the dust cloud.

After a few seconds his scream cuts off abruptly.

He's gone.

But you've got the mace, and it's a good weapon. You'll be able to do more damage with it, and be able to block an enemy's attack more effectively.

Go ahead and add one point to your Full Strength bubble, making it 9.

If you've been using pencil, you can probably just rub out any previous attributes and write in the new ones. But you can always use the back of your current character card if you need to (remember to copy the other information up too).

I know you're not at full strength at the moment (your strength is actually only 7 just now, because of the damage this very mace did you earlier), but don't worry about that. You'll be all healed up soon.

Because you chose a better weapon over your friend's life, your reputation goes down by 3. Go ahead and change it to 12.

The clubmen lie strewn across the desert like driftwood on a shore.

Five Twelve is buried in the collapsed mine shaft, along with the captain of these fallen guards (but at least his mace is safe and sound in your hands).

The other prisoners stare at you. The rain has washed the dirt and grime and sand off all of them, and you.

You know what they're thinking. You think it too.

Why did you let him die?

Not one of them speaks.

"Gather the water skins," you say. "Drink, all of you. Then fill them up with the rain, as full as you can."

They do so, no question.

One of them comes up to you. "We should say the words," he says. "For Five Twelve."

Your stomach knots. You nod. "What's your name?"

"Two Seven Two."

"Not your number. What's your name? Your real name."

He pauses, then shrugs. "Gord."

"Gourd? Like the vegetable?"

"I guess. But spelled differently. So they say. Not that I can write."

You nod. "Gord. Okay. Come on, then."

You prisoners stand in a line at the collapsed mine, and Gord wishes Five Twelve well in the next life, if there is such a place.

Go to page 28.

You gather the prisoners, and they stand in a semicircle around you, Gord in the middle.

"My name is Aquaan." You raise your voice above the rain. "And I'm an Elemental."

The group stirs. Someone mutters, "That explains the magic you used on them wolves."

Gord says, "You're one of the Eleven." This is barely a question.

You nod. "I'm one of the Eleven."

The tall one, Twenty-Three, asks, "Why haven't you used your magic before? You've been here months, haven't you?"

"Nearly a year. And I've been unable to use my power. I haven't got my staff..."

"Your *staff?*"

"Yes. I'm a water mage. I need a water source to be able to use my magic. My staff acts as that water source, so I'm able to cast whenever and wherever I want. But I've lost it. So until I get it back, I can only use magic when there's actual water about."

"Like now it's raining."

"Exactly. And there needs to be *enough* water. They give us a cup of water every day in our cells, but that's not enough."

Gord says, "You've been here nearly a *year.* The rest of the Eleven must think you're dead."

You swallow. "They might do. They probably sent someone to look for me, but they haven't really got any idea where I am. Last thing they knew I was fighting one of the monsters from Below. Unfortunately, that thing could fly, which I didn't realise. It carried me far over the mountains. And then it dropped me. I nearly died. And I lost my staff. And then a slave trader found me and sold me to Al'Nor."

The prisoners mutter amongst themselves, until Gord says, "So what now?"

Twenty-Three asks, "Do you think they know what's happened? The guards in the mine?"

You point to the iron gate you'd all walked through earlier. "There was a guard on that gate," you say. "He's not there anymore."

"He will have seen yer magic," says a man with a ginger beard, "and gone to get help."

"Then we can't stay here," says Gord.

"Agh, rubbish. Aquaan will just blast anyone who comes near, won't ye, Aquaan."

"It's not that easy," you say. "My powers are only just starting to come back. I'm not that strong yet."

"That ain't what I just saw."

"Well it's the truth. I won't be able to cast that spell again until I'm rested and my magic's replenished."

(That's true. See your **will** is down to 0 points, and *Arrow Rain* costs 6?)

"Then what do we do?"

"We should run," someone says. "I bet we can climb the canyon walls – they're not too steep in places."

"What, and take yer chance with the wolves?"

"It's not that simple," you say. "We're in the middle of nowhere. Does anyone really know where we are? Twenty-Three – you grew up in these mountains. Do *you* know where we are?"

He swallows. "Not really. Only that we're somewhere in the east of the Pan Valley. What I do know is, we're several days' walk from anywhere. And we don't have any food, and our water's going to run out by the end of the day."

"It's raining, ye fool," says the one with the ginger beard.

"*It won't rain forever.*"

You sigh. "We can't make it out there on foot. Not without food or water. We need the horses."

The prisoners exchange glances.

"The horses..." Gord says. "You mean *the* horses from the mine stables? Al'Nor's horses?"

And you nod. "I don't think we've got any other choice, have we? We need to go back through the gold mine."

CHAPTER FIVE:
Back Into The Freezer

They're not all happy about this suggestion, and who can blame them.

"I understand your concerns," you say, "but I think this is our best chance. It's our *only* chance. However, if anyone would prefer to leave now, that's completely up to you. I won't stop you."

The group of prisoners exchange glances. Mutter amongst themselves.

○ If you earlier chose to save Five Twelve, your reputation is currently at 17. You are well respected and trusted. Everyone stays to fight with you. **Add 3 points to your full strength bubble.**

○ If you earlier chose the mace over Five Twelve, your reputation is currently at 12. You are neither respected nor trusted, and a fair few prisoners do decide to leave and take their chances on their own. **Add 1 point to your full strength bubble.**

Next thing. You are not at full strength nor full will. You can replenish your attributes by completing this five times table test.

The Five Times Table					
1x5=5	2x5=10	3x5=15	4x5=20	5x5=25	6x5=30
7x5=35	8x5=40	9x5=45	10x5=50	11x5=55	12x5=60

Cover the answers on page 31. Now take the test, answering on scrap paper. This one's easier, so you need to get 19 or more correct. You have **90 seconds**.

THE TEST				
1)5x5= 25	2)9x5= 45	3)2x5= 10	4)7x5=35	5)8x5=40
6)3x5= 15	7)12x5= 60	8)11x5=55	9)6x5=30	10)5x5= 25
11)1x5= 5	12)8x5= 40	13)3x5= 15	14)12x5=60	15)4x5= 20
16)10x5=50	17)2x5= 10	18)6x5=30	19)9x5=45	20)12x5=60

Uncover the answers on page 31 and mark it. If you got 19 or more, your strength and will scores fully replenish. Rub out the *0* in your **will** box and write in *6*, which is your full will score. Now do the same with your strength, writing in your full strength attribute. If you did not get 19 or 20, you should retake the test.

Your will is replenished. You don't have enough will points for Vortex, but Arrow Rain is back on the table! And you're back to full strength, too.

It's time to invade the gold mine. That means you will be out of the rain. You take a long drink and then fill up your water skin with rain water until it's fit to burst. *This* water skin will act as a water source. There's enough to cast one spell and to heal yourself too.

Write **water skin x1** under *items* on your character card.

"How do we get back inside?" Gord asks. "The gate won't budge." He's trying to lift it with his bare hands.

"Can you reach the winch lever?"

"No..."

"I know where we need to go," you say, and when everyone turns to you you point down the collapsed mine shaft. "There. That'll lead us back into the mine."

No one can argue with that logic.

You lead your ragtag band over to the hole. "We can climb down the landslide. Just be careful not to slip."

You try not to think of the bodies, both wolf and human, beneath the debris as you scale down the rock face. It's slippy with loose sand and rain, but you all make it down in one piece.

Light from the hole above you illuminates much of the shaft. After just a couple of minutes of walking you see the mineshaft split into three tunnels.

"We need to pick one that's not abandoned," Twenty-Three says, "so there are wall torches on the wall, or else it's going to get very dark very quickly."

"How are we s'post to tell the blinkin difference? They all look the same."

"I know which one we need to pick," says Gord. "*The freezer.* It's the only shaft on this side of the mine that's still being worked."

"Well how are we supposed to know which one's *the freezer?*"

"We can work it out."

It's lucky Twenty-Three grew up in these mountains. You can use his knowledge to discover the correct mineshaft to take. Cool, huh?

  Below is a number line. It includes negative numbers. It will help you answer the following questions. But first, **cover the answers on the opposite page**!

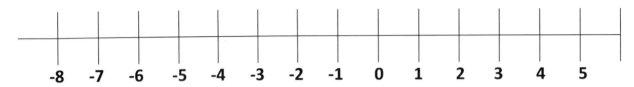

-8   -7   -6   -5   -4   -3   -2   -1   0   1   2   3   4   5

Exercises

1] Work out the following.

a) $0 - 3 =$ **b)** $2 - 5 =$ **c)** $-1 - 6 =$ **d)** $-4 - 2 =$

e) $-4 + 1 =$ **f)** $-1 + 3 =$ **g)** $-8 + 11 =$ **h)** $-6 + 4 =$

2] Twenty-Three points to a mossy plant growing in the mineshaft you're currently standing in. "It's mountain lichen," he says. "This plant only grows at temperatures of 5°c." So this mineshaft must be **5°c**.

a) Tunnel 1 is **6 degrees cooler** than your current mineshaft (which is 5°c). What is the temperature of Tunnel 1?

b) Tunnel 2 is **11 degrees cooler** than your current mineshaft (which is 5°c). What is the temperature of Tunnel 2?

c) Tunnel 3 is **7 degrees cooler than Tunnel 1**. What is its temperature?

Twenty-Three says that he once overheard a guard say that *the freezer* is -6°c. So which is the correct tunnel?

Now check and mark your answers using page 33. How did you do? If you made any mistakes, try and work out where you went wrong.

  Add **1 point** to your full strength and **1 point** to your full speed.

Go to page 34.

NEGATIVE NUMBERS: Answers

1]

a) -3   **b)** -3   **c)** -7   **d)** -6

e) -3   **f)** 2   **g)** 3   **h)** -2

2]

a) $5 - 6 = -1$

b) $5 - 11 = -6$

c) $-1 - 7 = -8$

The correct tunnel, known as *the freezer*, is **Tunnel 2**.

You decide between you that the middle tunnel must be *the freezer*, and sure enough before long you see flickering wall torches further ahead.

"Ah, good job, Twenty-Three," you say. "And good work everyone."

It *is* freezing though. The walls sparkle with ice crystals, except for a dry halo around each flickering torch. A few of the prisoners shiver, but you don't feel the cold like people do. An advantage of being one of the Eleven.

As you walk past a subsidiary tunnel on your left, every single one of you looks at the unmovable blockage plugging the shaft. The story is well-known to all of you. A cave-in years before had trapped thirteen people – nine prisoners, four guards – inside a dead-end mine. Rescuers had tried to dig them out. But when they'd caused a second cave-in (crushing one of their party), Al'Nor had reluctantly called off the rescue.

One of the trapped guards had been the previous High Protector. After the accident, Caesar had been promoted to the position.

As far as anyone knows, the bodies are still there.

When I've enough will to perform Vortex again, you think, *I'll be able to shift that blockage.*

Vortex is a powerful spell, but just too much for you at the moment. At some point, however, you'll be able to perform it again. You can then come back here at **any time** and blast the blockage out of the way. If you remember, that is. You'll have to have a water skin as a water source, mind. Then simply turn to **page 83** (again, at any time, as long as you can perform *Vortex*) to see what's beyond.

For now, you carry on past the blockage, back through *the freezer* until you reach the rock-hewn staircase and start to climb. Up and up you lead the other prisoners – the *freed* prisoners – until you reach the top of the staircase and the anteroom outside the cell block.

To your left is the staircase you climbed barely an hour ago on your way to The Pit. Straight ahead is the tunnel leading to the abandoned *ice box*. And to your right is the closed, locked iron door of the cell block.

Gord tries the handle. "Locked. We need a key."

"Well who has a key?"

"Who flippin cares?" interjects the ginger-bearded prisoner you are starting to think of as The Ginger Whinger. "I say we just get the hell outta this place. Now. Just take the hosses and go."

"*Horses*. Not *hosses*," Gord scolds. He turns back to you. "The guard captains have keys to the cell block."

"Pity you buried our guard captain under a tonne of rubble then," says Twenty-Three, but he has a wry smile on his face.

"Okay," you say. "Can't do anything about that here. Let's go. Up."

CHAPTER SIX:
The Stables

You lead your ragtag band up the staircase, past the entrances to the mine shafts – past the one that you'd been led through earlier on the way to The Pit.

"Stay alert," you say, as if they need reminding.

The flickering torches cast a little light, but then about five minutes into your ascent that all stops.

"They've extinguished the torches."

All of them, from that point on. Nothing but pitch black. "Take one off the wall," you say, hoisting the nearest one out of its sconce and holding it aloft.

"They're going to see us coming a mile off," someone mutters.

"Well it's either this or we're blind."

The stairs open out suddenly into a chamber. Too suddenly. Perhaps if the place had been better lit you'd have seen them coming. As it is, three guards jump you as you enter the small room.

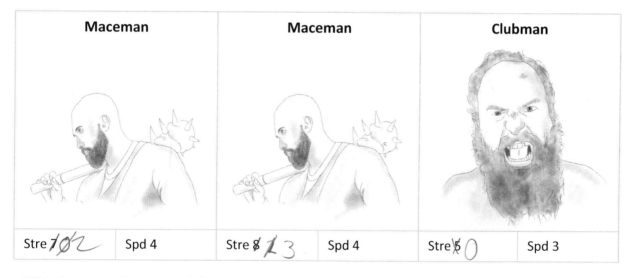

Maceman		Maceman		Clubman	
Stre 1 Ø 2	Spd 4	Stre 8 1 3	Spd 4	Stre 5 0	Spd 3

This is a sneak attack. The one in the middle attacks you first, so you barely have time to react, and you can't use your magic. Reduce your strength accordingly. You know how it works now. His strength (8) minus your speed (6) = how much damage you take (2). After he's attacked, it's your turn (they can't *all* sneak attack you at the same time). So choose carefully. Then play out the rest of the battle.

When they're defeated, you can pick up a fallen mace **if you haven't already got one**, and add 1 to your full strength bubble. If you already have a mace, don't pick up another one, you greedy piggy, and don't add anything to your full strength.

"Everyone alright?"

"Well, we're alive."

"Are *you* alright?" Gord asks, looking at the wound you took. He sucks his teeth. "Ssss – that looks bad..."

"I didn't see him coming. Just give me a sec. Watch that no one else is going to surprise us."

You can heal yourself with your magic, and you only need a little water, so **do not** cross off your water skin. Don't spill any either, will you?

To activate your magic and heal yourself, complete this six times table test. First, cover the answers at the bottom of the page. I'm trusting you not to be a Cheaty Von Cheatface.

The Six Times Table					
1x6=6	2x6=12	3x6=18	4x6=24	5x6=30	6x6=36
7x6=42	8x6=48	9x6=54	10x6=60	11x6=66	12x6=72

You have **90 seconds**. Again, answer on a scrap piece of paper and then check your answers below. If you get 18 or more you return to full strength. If you get 16 or 17, your strength *mostly* replenishes. Knock one point off your full strength. That's what your strength is now.

THE TEST

1)5x6= 30	2)9x6= 54	3)2x6= 12	4)7x6= 42	5)8x6= 48
6)3x6= 18	7)12x6= 72	8)11x6= 66	9)6x6= 36	10)5x6= 30
11)1x6= 6	12)8x6= 48	13)3x6= 18	14)12x6= 72	15)4x6= 24
16)10x6= 60	17)2x6= 12	18)6x6= 36	19)9x6= 54	20)12x6= 72

You heal yourself, and the wound closes and seals right before their eyes. This predictably brings murmurs of wonder from your ragtag band.

"Wish I could do that."

"Me too."

"If we cut off yer leg, would it grow back?"

You don't listen to any of them. You've looked around the small chamber and brought your torch up to the gate in one wall, inspecting the padlock, which is hooked between the gate post and wall grill, clamping it shut.

"It needs a code. There're six digits."

The Ginger Whinger says, "Can we guess it?"

"Well given that there's literally a million possibilities – no."

"Can't ye just snap it in two?"

"Don't you think I've tried?"

"Perhaps one of these guards wrote the code on the back of their hand or something," says Twenty-Three, bending down to have a look.

"It's not going to be that easy," you say, and give the padlock another tug.

"What are we going to do then?" asks Gord.

"How long would it take to try all them different possibilities?"

You sigh. "Well, say by some miracle we could try a thousand combinations in an hour. How many hours would it take to try a million combinations?"

The Ginger Whinger looks lost, so you add, "There are a thousand thousands in a million."

"Right..."

"So it would take *a thousand hours*."

"Oh."

"Hey, I found something." Everyone turns to look at Twenty-Three.

"Do not tell me there's a six digit number written on the back of one of their hands."

"No, but I found this sheet of paper in this one's pocket. I think they're clues."

Worksheet Topic 3
POWERS OF 10 | ROUNDING | ROMAN NUMERALS

Some worksheets also double up as **checkpoints**. You will return to a checkpoint if you ever fall in battle (that is, when your strength is reduced to zero). Your attributes then fully replenish. Checkpoints also offer extra, optional exercises. You can continue with the story after completing the main exercise – or, if you wish, you can do the extra questions to further improve your attributes.

If/when you do fall in battle, return to the previous checkpoint and complete any extra questions you skipped. This will make you stronger, ready for when you have to reface the enemy. If you've already completed the extra exercises at one checkpoint, go back to the *previous checkpoint* and complete those extra questions. If you have no extra questions to complete, you *will* be strong enough to win. Just try again.

POWERS OF 10

A **one** followed by any number of **zeros** is a *power of 10.* These numbers are all examples of powers of 10: **10   100   1000   10 000   100 000**

"Counting in powers of 10" sounds complicated, but it's not, not really. It simply means adding or subtracting 10, or 100, or 1000 (or any other power of 10) each time.

Exercises

1] Fill in the missing numbers in these exercises.
a) **Count on** (this means **add**) in steps of 10 000, starting from 0.

| 0 | 10 000 | 20 000 | 30 000 | 40 000 | 50 000 | 60 000 |

b) **Count on** in steps of 100 000, staring from 230 350.

| 230 350 | 330 350 | 430 350 | 530 350 | 630 350 | 730 350 |

c) Count back (this means **subtract**) in steps of 100. Start at 6300.

6300   6200   6100...   6000...   5900...   5800

d) Count back in steps of 1 000 000, starting from 6 750 001.

6 750 001   5 750 001   4 750 001.   3 750 001   2 750 001

2] The first two digits of the padlock is the **3ʳᵈ step** in the following sequence:
Count back in steps of 10, starting from 116.

116   106....   ...96....   ...86...

Check your answers on page 41, then add **1 point** to your full strength.

ROUNDING

This is what you have to work out when rounding a number:

- The number lies between two possible answers.
- You have to decide which answer the number is closest to.

Remember your place values: **Ten Thousands | Thousands | Hundreds | Tens | Ones**
    You will be rounding *"to the nearest ten"*, or *"to the nearest hundred"*, or *"to the nearest thousand"* etc.
    The **decider** is the digit to the *right* of the place you're rounding to. For instance, if you're rounding *"to the nearest ten"*, the decider is the *Ones* digit. If you're rounding *"to the nearest ten thousand"*, the decider is the *Thousands* digit. And so on.
    If the decider is 5 or more, round up. If the decider is less than 5, round down.

Exercises

1] Round these numbers **to the nearest ten** (the *Tens* digits are highlighted). The **decider** is the *Ones* digit. The first two are done for you.

a) 67 becomes **70**, because the decider is greater than 5.
b) 83 becomes **80**, because the decider is less than 5.

c) 28   **d) 6**2   **e) 4**9   **f) 6**3

2] Round these numbers **to the nearest hundred**. Remember, we are now rounding the *Hundreds* digit, and the *Tens* digit is the decider.

a) **3**90   b) 562   c) 692   d) 237

3] Round this number **to the nearest hundred thousand**. First, circle the *Hundred Thousand* digit. Then use the decider to round up or down.

679 078   rounded to the nearest hundred thousand: .7̶0̶0̶.̶0̶0̶0̶ . . .

4] Round this two digit number **to the nearest ten** and you'll get the 3rd and 4th digits of the padlock.

48 rounded to the nearest ten: . . 4̶0̶ . . . .

Check your answers on p41, then add **1 point** to your full speed.

ROMAN NUMERALS

The ten digits we use today – 0, 1, 2, 3, 4, 5, 6, 7, 8, 9 – are called *Arabic numerals*. These were adopted in Europe in the Middle Ages. Previously, Europe used *Roman numerals*, with numbers represented by letters.

I = 1   V = 5   X = 10   L = 50   C = 100   D = 500   M = 1000

- **Add together** any repeated numerals sitting next to each other in a row:

  III = 3   XX = 20   CCC = 300   MM = 2000

- Small numerals **after** bigger numerals are **added** to the bigger one:

  VI = 6   VIII = 8   XII = 12   CIII = 103   CCXXX = 230

- Small numerals **before** bigger numerals are **subtracted** from the bigger one:

  IV = 4   IX = 9   XL = 40   XC = 90   LD = 450   CM = 900

- Do any **subtracting before** any adding!

1] Write the following Roman numerals in our familiar 0-9 numbers. There are no small numbers before big ones, so all you have to do is add them.

a) CCXV = 215   **b)** MCCLII = 1252

c) MMC = 2100   **d)** LXXV = 75   **e)** CCCLXII = 362   **f)** DCIII = 603

2] The following Roman numerals *do* have smaller numbers before big ones. Make sure you do the subtracting *first*.

a) MMLM = 250   **b)** MCM = 1900   **c)** MCMLXVIII = 1968

d) CDXL = 440   **e)** MMXIV = 2014   **f)** MCMXCIV = 1994

3] The last two digits on the padlock are represented by this Roman numeral:

XCVIII = ..98...

Check your answers on page 42 and add **1 point** to your full will. Then you have a choice. You can either carry on with the story (go to page 43) or if you wish you may complete the extra exercises for an extra reward (go to page 42).

POWERS OF 10: Answers

1] a) 0   10 000   20 000   30 000   40 000   50 000   60 000
b) 230 350   330 350   430 350   530 350   630 350   730 350
c) 6300   6200   6100   6000   5900   5800
d) 6 750 001   5 750 001   4 750 001   3 750 001   2 750 001

2]   116   106   96   .. 86 ..

ROUNDING: Answers

1] c) 30   **d)** 60   **e)** 50   **f)** 60

2] a) 400   **b)** 600   **c)** 700   **d)** 200

3]   679 078 rounded to the nearest hundred thousand: **700 000**

4]   48 rounded to the nearest ten: . . . 50 . .

1] c) MMC = 2100   **d)** LXXV = 75   **e)** CCCLXII = 362   **f)** DCIII = 603

2] d) CDXL = 440   **e)** MMXIV = 2014   **f)** MCMXCIV = 1994

3] XCVIII = ... 98 ...

EXTRA EXERCISES

First, cover the answers, which are at the bottom of the page!

1] a) From **20 563**, <u>count on</u> in steps of **100**. Stop at **20 963**.

20 563   .20663..   .20763.   20863.   ..20963

b) From **121 012**, <u>count down</u> in steps of **10 000**. Stop after four steps.

121 012   .111.012..   .101012   .91.012..   ...81.012

2] Round the following numbers to the nearest **hundred**.

a) 650   **b)** 1230   **c)** 972   **d)** 12 051   **e)** 101
700   1000   1000   12 100   100

3] Write these numbers as Roman numerals.

a) 27   **b)** 152   **c)** 2461
XXVII   CLII   MMCDLXI

Now check your answers below. Add **1 point** to your full speed and replenish your attributes. Now go to page 43.

1] a) 20 563   20 663   20 763   20 863   20 963

b) 121 012   111 012   101 012   91 012   81 012

2] a) 700   **b)** 1200   **c)** 1000   **d)** 12 100   **e)** 100

3] a) XXVII   **b)** CLII   **c)** MMCDLXI

You input the numbers – 865098 – and the padlock clicks and falls away. You look at Twenty-Three, who nods at you. "Good work," you tell him, and ease open the gate, which squeaks and squeals.

There's a ramp leading up, twisting around on itself like a bobsleigh run. You creep up, hugging the wall. At the top of the ramp is an open gate, through which you can see a large courtyard open to the sky, and a wall made up of wooden spikes.

It is still raining.

"*Extinguish your torches!*" you hiss, and everyone does so, underfoot.

"What have we got?" Gord joins your side, hunkered down in the shadows.

"Guards. A lot of them."

They are running about, this way and that.

You will need your magic for this.

Activate your magic by completing this test on the seven times table.

The Seven Times Table					
1x7=7	2x7=14	3x7=21	4x7=28	5x7=35	6x7=42
7x7=49	8x7=56	9x7=63	10x7=70	11x7=77	12x7=84

You have **90 seconds**. Answer on a scrap piece of paper. You should put this paper over the answers, covering them whilst you complete the test. Then check them. If you get 16 or more you may use your magic. If not, you need to retake it.

THE TEST				
1)5x7= 35	2)9x7=63	3)2x7=14	4)7x7=49	5)8x7=56
6)3x7=21	7)12x7=84	8)11x7=77	9)6x7=42	10)5x7=35
11)1x7=7	12)8x7=56	13)3x7=21	14)12x7=84	15)4x7=28
16)10x7=70	17)2x7=14	18)6x7=42	19)9x7=63	20)12x7=84

ANSWERS						
1) 35	2) 63	3) 14	4) 49	5) 56	6) 21	7) 84
8) 77	9) 42	10) 35	11) 7	12) 56	13) 21	14) 84
15) 28	16) 70	17) 14	18) 42	19) 63	20) 84	

You have the rain as a water source, so you don't need to use your water skin.

You venture slowly up the ramp. You can see one wooden watchtower built into the wall. Half a dozen archers stand in it, getting soaked.

There are a few isolated guards crossing the courtyard, and then a group of four standing close together.

Arrow Rain would be effective against this group, and it would also be effective against the archers in the watchtower. But you won't have the time or will to cast it twice. You need to choose which group to assault. Think carefully.

○ To cast *Arrow Rain* against the archers in the watchtower, **go to page 47.**

○ To cast *Arrow Rain* against the group of guards on the courtyard floor, **carry on reading.**

The archers can wait. This group of guards is a more pressing concern. You summon your water magic, yell, "With me!" and run out into the courtyard.

Power surges through you, and the rain hisses as it hits your skin.

You throw your hands up, and the rain morphs into scything blades, and then down it comes, at your direction, onto the group of guards who haven't yet had time to react. Take 6 hit points away from each one.

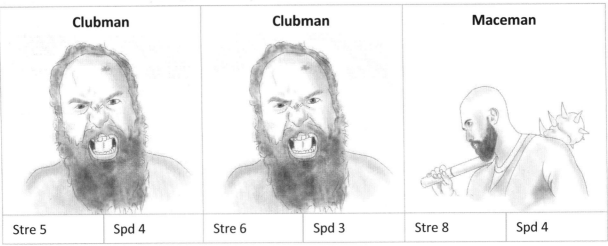

Clubman		**Clubman**		**Maceman**	
Stre 5	Spd 4	Stre 6	Spd 3	Stre 8	Spd 4

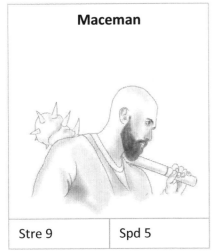

Maceman

Stre 9	Spd 5

The two clubmen fall. The macemen survive, just about, but you can despatch them easily.

By this time, though, the archers in the tower have nocked their arrows, and they fire on you and your ragtag band.

You are able to duck out of the way, but two of your gang fall, and there is nothing you can do for them.

"We're sitting ducks!" Gord cries.

"Into the tunnel!" You lead them back under the portcullis and a little way down the ramp, breathing heavily.

You have lost two men. Reduce your **full strength** by 1.

Because you made that bad decision, you must also reduce your reputation by 1.

Adjust your character card now.

"Why didn't you take out the archers first?" asks Twenty-Three, which is easy to ask now, in hindsight.

"Can you use your magic again?" Gord looks back up the ramp to the courtyard. You are out of view of the archers now, but the surviving guards must be discussing their attack.

You need to replenish your will *and* then activate your magic to do so. A huge effort, meaning you need to complete this larger than normal times table challenge. You have **2 minutes** this time. Again, cover the answers below with your scrap piece of paper.

You need at least 26, else you'll have to do it again.

THE TEST

1)5x4= 20
2)9x6= 54
3)2x7= 14
4)9x2= 18
5)8x5= 40
6)3x10= 30
7)12x4= 48
8)11x3= 33
9)6x3= 18
10)5x6= 30
11)1x7= 7
12)8x2= 16
13)3x1= 3
14)12x6= 72
15)4x6= 24
16)10x10= 100
17)2x5= 10
18)6x6= 36
19)9x7= 63
20)12x5= 60
21)5x3= 15
22)9x4= 36
23)2x7= 8
24)7x6= 4
25)8x2= 16
26)3x6= 18
27)12x7= 84
28)11x5= 55
29)6x5= 30
30)4x7= 28

ANSWERS

1) 20	2) 54	3) 14	4) 18	5) 40	6) 30	7) 48
8) 33	9) 18	10) 30	11) 7	12) 16	13) 3	14) 72
15) 24	16) 100	17) 10	18) 36	19) 63	20) 60	21) 15
22) 36	23) 14	24) 42	25) 16	26) 18	27) 84	28) 55
29) 30	30) 28					

Finally, your magic is back, and you're able to blast the watchtower, screaming with the effort as you do so. The force is so strong the watchtower actually collapses under the barrage, falling to the courtyard in a crash of splintering wood, the archers going with it.

And then the remaining guards, the ones who had just been milling about — there're three of them and they are on top of you. You don't have the time or strength to summon your magic again, so you'll have to beat them hand-to-hand. Luckily you are the faster, and so you can attack one of them first. Then they take their turns from left to right.

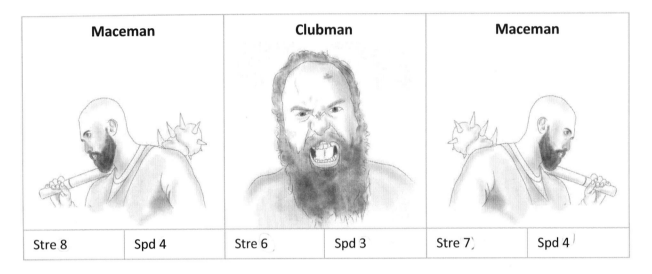

Maceman		Clubman		Maceman	
Stre 8	Spd 4	Stre 6	Spd 3	Stre 7	Spd 4

Remember, if you lose the battle, return to checkpoint 1 and complete the extra exercises on page 42, if you haven't already. If you've already completed them, you *will* be strong enough to beat these enemies. Just try again.

Otherwise, the courtyard is now clear.

Go to page 49.

It's a no-brainer.

If you don't take out the archers in the watchtower now, they'll be able to fire on you. You summon your water magic, yell, "With me!" and run out into the courtyard. Power surges through you, and the rain hisses as it hits your skin.

You throw your hands up, and the rain morphs into scything blades, and then down it comes, at your direction, onto the watchtower and the archers inside. There are screams, and the sounds of splintering wood. The force is so great that the watchtower collapses, falling to the courtyard with a crash, taking the archers down with it.

You don't have the time or energy to use your magic again, so you charge the group of guards, yelling your ragtag band do the same.

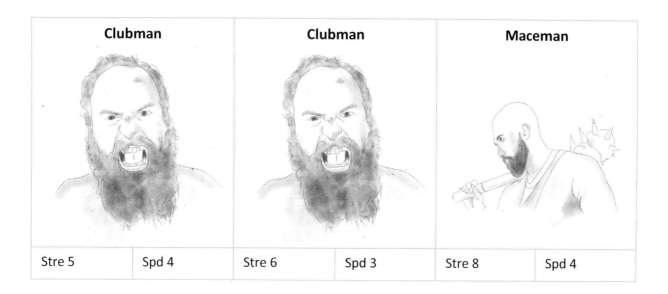

Clubman		Clubman		Maceman	
Stre 5	Spd 4	Stre 6	Spd 3	Stre 8	Spd 4

Maceman

Stre 9	Spd 5

You are faster than all of them, so can attack first. Choose your victim carefully. They then take their turns, one at a time, from left to right. Then your go again. If you lose the battle, return to checkpoint 1 and complete the extra exercises on page 42.

You've only just defeated that bunch when the remaining guards close in on you from their spots on the courtyard. You haven't had time to heal yourself, so your attributes stay as they are.

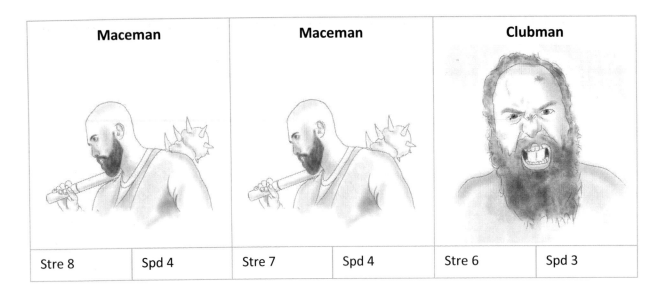

Maceman		Maceman		Clubman	
Stre 8	Spd 4	Stre 7	Spd 4	Stre 6	Spd 3

Again, if you lose the battle, complete the extra exercises on 42. If you've already completed them, you *will* be strong enough to beat these enemies. Just try again.

Otherwise, the courtyard is now clear.

Go to page 49.

The courtyard is eerily quiet under the drumming of the rain, which has faded into the background.

Heal yourself by completing this test.

The Eight Times Table

1x8=8	2x8=16	3x8=24	4x8=32	5x8=40	6x8=48
7x8=56	8x8=64	9x8=72	10x8=80	11x8=88	12x8=96

You have **90 seconds**, as normal. Answer on a scrap piece of paper, covering the answers below. If you get 18 or more your strength, speed and will replenish fully. If you get 16 or 17 they replenish *almost* completely – subtract 1 from your full strength, speed and will. That's the number they replenish to.

THE TEST

1)5x8=	2)9x8=	3)2x8=	4)7x8=	5)8x8=
6)3x8=	7)12x8=	8)11x8=	9)6x8=	10)5x8=
11)1x8=	12)8x8=	13)3x8=	14)12x8=	15)4x8=
16)10x8=	17)2x8=	18)6x8=	19)9x8=	20)12x8=

ANSWERS

1) 40	2) 72	3) 16	4) 56	5) 64	6) 24	7) 96
8) 88	9) 48	10) 40	11) 8	12) 64	13) 24	14) 96
15) 32	16) 80	17) 16	18) 48	19) 72	20) 96	

If you are disappointed in your result, simply retake the test.

"The stables, then," says The Ginger Whinger, "before more of em come."

You cross the courtyard, holding your mace high, listening and looking out for any sign of movement.

You can hear the horses, and smell them, too. "That building there."

It's a large stone structure with wooden stalls and a wooden roof, and the ground outside is littered with matted hay. To the right of the stables is the main gate, which is open.

"Stay alert."

As you get closer, one of the stable doors bursts open, and out thunders a guard on horseback. The horse rears as it sees you, its front legs kicking the air. Then the guard gets his steed back under control and urges it in the direction of the gate.

He is fleeing. Fleeing from you.

Then you recognise his leather helmet.

He's a guard captain.

You throw your mace. Hard. It's a beautiful shot. Hits him square on the back of his head.

The guard slumps forward and then topples off his horse, which runs straight out the gate without a rider.

You retrieve your mace and roll the captain onto his back. He is unconscious.

Gord knows what you are thinking. "He has his key on him?"

He does. You find it in his belt bag and hold it up. "The key to the cell block."

CHAPTER SEVEN:

Who Are We?

"We should g ___ the prisoners," says Gord.

The Ginge ___ serious? The gate is *right there*. Open! Let's take the hoss ___

"How do ___ nymore?" Gord looks at you then, as if for supp ___ . Monsters, they said. Monsters that come out o ___

The Gin ___ *stories...*"

"They'r ___ monsters are real. I've seen them. I've *fought* the ___ *or*. To fight them."

No on ___ *y*'ve seen what you can do. They know *you're* rea ___ onsters?

"Ther ___ eone else says, "way before I ended up here. T ___ Pole. Sea monsters sinking ships in the Great (___ ngowa and the deserts of Lore."

"Yes ___ onsters came to the mountains of Sha'Pan. Here, ___ d I fought one, and it almost killed me. That's ___ here. It's how I lost my staff. The sad fact is – w ___ here anymore. We... we don't even know if your l ___

Ag ___ er Whinger says, "Well, there's only one way to fi ___ e." He turns and heads to the stables. "I ain't dyin ___ . "I've been ere long enough!"

G ___ er him, but you shake your head. "Leave him."

"I ___ em, right? The others? I mean, *who are we* if we leav ___

Wh—

That's when ___ er trots his horse out of the stables, kicks it into a gallop and disappears through the gate without another word.

"Aquaan? We're going back for them, right?"

○ To go back inside the mine and unlock the cell block, **go to page 54.**

○ To abandon the rest of the prisoners, take a horse and go, **turn to page 52.**

(character sheet card overlay)

Lucy

	Full:	
Strength	4	2 8 7 9 10 11
Speed	2	5 6 7 8 9 10
Will	0	5 6 2 3
Reputation	4	6
		15 12

Spells: ARROW RAIN   Cost: 6 will   Damage 6 to **all** enemies in battle

VORTEX   Cost: 8 will   Damage 12 to **one** enemy

Items: Mother Skinx?

"I'm sorry, Gord," you say. "I... I'm needed elsewhere."

He frowns, startled. "*What?*"

"You don't understand what's happening out in the world. The rest of the Eleven need me. I don't have time to stay here."

"I can't believe it..." Gord looks at you like you're a completely alien life form. "I can't believe you're a *coward*. An Elemental. And you're a coward."

"I'm not a coward..."

"Give me the key." He glares at you, holding out his palm. "The key to the cell block. Give it to me. If you won't come we'll do it without you." And he looks at the other prisoners. "Won't we."

Some of them shuffle a bit, but Twenty-Three goes and stands next to Gord with no hesitation. Eventually, most of your ragtag band has crossed over and stands with Gord. You are left with just a few men. All are looking at the floor.

You hand over the key. "I'm sorry," you say. "I'm not a hero."

"Then what's the point of you?" Gord takes the key and leads his men back towards the mine.

You lose 2 reputation points.

You say to the others, "Come on," and head into the stables.

Your stomach is all knotted, but you don't think Gord has been exactly fair. He doesn't realise what Numera is facing. If he knew what you'd done, what sacrifices you'd made, the lives you'd already saved, well maybe he'd actually give you some of the respect you deserve!

The men who are leaving with you take the nearest horses and go.

You want the strongest steed you can get, so you inspect each stall. And in the furthest one, cowering in the corner, in the hay, is the stable girl.

She is perhaps twelve. Dirty. Frightened, with wild eyes. She's covered in straw. She gasps when she sees you, and tries to back further away.

"I'm not going to hurt you," you say with a sigh.

"I saw what you did..." she mumbles. "You can use magic..."

You nod. "I can."

"You're one of the Eleven."

"Yes."

"I knew you existed. Me brother and me used to argue about it. He didn't think you was real. But then he saw that staff..."

You freeze. "What did you say?"

"That staff." She nods at you. "He told me he saw a staff, a magic one, with blue glowing smoke in it. And he started to believe after all. It's yours, ain't it."

"When was this?" you ask, and now your stomach is churning. "*Where* was this?"

"Only a couple of months ago. And he saw it *here*, in the courtyard. A trader gave it to Al'Nor hisself."

Al'Nor has my staff.

You don't say another word to the stable girl. You turn round and stride out of the stables. Excitement is bubbling in your belly. Excitement and abject rage, that your staff is in the hands of that disgusting old man.

Gord and the others are crowded at the entrance to the ramp. They hear you coming and turn round.

"Aquaan?"

You take a deep breath through your nose. "Give me the key back, Gord."

"You're coming with us?"

"Yes. I've just found out AL'Nor has my staff. I want it back."

Go to page 55.

"Of course we're going back for them."

Gord doesn't quite smile, but he nods.

You look around. "Take a horse and go after The Ginger Whinger if you wish."

Someone says, "I'm not sure that's his name..."

"But imagine it was the other way round," you continue. "Imagine *you* were stuck in the cells. You'd want us to come rescue you, right? So let's go rescue them."

Your reputation goes up by 1 point.

Your ragtag band doesn't exactly cheer, but they all look at each other and nod. And no one wants to be like The Ginger Whinger and leave, and disappoint the memory of their ancestors and disgrace their family name, if they can even remember it.

"Come with me."

On the way back to the gate and the ramp, you hear movement under a nearby hay wagon, and when you look under it you see the stable boy. He is perhaps ten, hiding in the dirt with grease and hay plastered to his forehead. He gasps at you.

"It's okay," you say. "I'm not going to hurt you. Come out of there."

The boy does as he's told, his wide eyes never leaving you for even a second.

"Where do you live?" you ask, and he just points towards the gate, which you take as *out there somewhere*. "You should go home, lad."

You start walking past him when he says, "I saw what you did. You got magic in you. You're an *emma...* an *emma-nem...* Emmental."

"Emmental is a cheese."

"I seen your staff."

That stops you. It almost floors you, truth be told. You turn back to the stable boy. "What did you say?"

"It *is* yours, isn't it. I didn't think you people was real until I saw yer staff. Me sister always believed, but she's a dummy."

You try not to get too excited. "W-why do you think it was my staff?"

"It was magic!" The boy's eyes light up and he grins. "It had blue magic smoke in it, swirling around like this..." and he makes a whirligig with one finger.

You suck in a long, slow breath. "Where did you see it?"

"*Here*, in this courtyard. Coupla months back. A trader gave it to Al'Nor hisself."

Al'Nor has my staff.

Excitement bubbles in your belly. Excitement and abject rage, that your staff is in the hands of that disgusting old man.

"Go home," you tell the boy. "It's not safe here."

"You're telling me! I gotta get me sister." And he runs off through the rain in the direction of the stables.

Go to page 55.

"Your *staff?*" Gord asks.

"It's magic. Each Elemental has one. It acts as a source for our power. So my staff acts as a water source."

"What does that mean?"

"It means I can use my magic even if there's not any *actual water* about."

Twenty-Three chuckles. "That would have come in handy back down there."

"Yep."

"And now Al'Nor has it," Gord says. "Can he even use it? The magic, I mean?"

"Nope. Only a... only someone like me can use it."

"An Elemental."

You shrug. *Not exactly.* "If you like."

"Well at least that's something. At least he hasn't got magic powers too, on top of all his guards."

Well, that's true.

You approach the ramp leading down into the mines, and you sigh. "Ah."

"Portcullis is down," Twenty-Three says, just in case you're blind.

"Is there another way in? Another way round?"

"Well there's nothing that way," Gord says, pointing back past the stables. "Just that massive canyon we were stuck at the bottom of earlier."

"What about this way?" You lead them past the closed gate to the other end of the courtyard. Built into the mountainside is a stone hut, with a dozen steps leading up to it.

"It's the gatehouse."

"Maybe there'll be another way in."

Gord says, "Well hopefully there'll be a way to open the gate."

You shrug. "Maybe."

"Clue's in the name."

"We can only give it a try." You lead them up the steps with your mace held aloft. The stone hut has no windows and a solid wooden door, which you kick down. It splinters off its hinges and dances across the room before falling flat.

The gatehouse is empty.

"Clear," you say, heading into the dingy room, allowing your eyes adjust. "No one's here."

There's a table, a wall cupboard and chest of drawers, and then a solid metal door that appears to lead directly into the mountain. This door is locked. You can't kick it down, either; it's too strong.

"Nope," you say. "Won't budge."

"Hey, look at this." One of the others has opened a drawer and withdrawn a yellowed sheet of paper. It's a map of the gold mine.

"This will come in handy."

It shows the mineshafts, spread out like a cobweb, and also the cell block, the armoury, healing bay, food store and well, the barracks, and also Al'Nor's vast residence built into the mountainside.

"It's like a castle. He lives in a castle," someone says.

"Looks like this leads right to it," you say, pointing to the locked metal door behind you.

"But there's another way up to his place here, Aquaan. From *below*. Through the cell block and out the other side. Follow this passageway here, and just head *up*. Past the food store, past the barracks..."

"He lives *above* the barracks. Of course he does."

"...up this staircase, round and round, and you can reach his residence from below."

"This is the way Al'Nor always comes down to the cells, isn't it," you say, tracing your finger. "Down and down, underground..."

"Like a mole."

"Like a *rat*."

"...picks his guards up from the barracks, heads through these tunnels and comes through *this* door into the cell block, like he did this morning, rather than the one we left by to get to the mine shafts."

"There's loads of things that way," says Gord. "The armoury, healing bay, barracks, food store, well..."

"Well? Well what?" asks Twenty-Three.

"A *well* well, you idiot," one of the other prisoners laughs. "As in a well for getting water?"

"There's an underground river in the caves beneath this mountain, isn't there," you say.

You roll up the map. "We'll take this."

"Hey, what do you think this is?"

One of the other prisoners has opened the wall cupboard.

It is in the corner next to the door leading back out into the courtyard and the rain.

It is a cog with a metal chain, which heads out through slats in the wall.

"It's a pulley," you say, coming over. "For the portcullis."

"It won't budge." The prisoner tries to move it, but it's locked in place.

Worksheet Topic 4
SQUARE & CUBE NUMBERS | MULTIPLES

SQUARE & CUBE NUMBERS

A **square number** is simply a number multiplied by itself. You already know 12 of them, thanks to your times tables. Let's write them out:

1]

$1 \times 1 = \ldots$ $2 \times 2 = \ldots$ $3 \times 3 = \ldots$ $4 \times 4 = \ldots$

$5 \times 5 = \ldots$ $6 \times 6 = \ldots$ $7 \times 7 = \ldots$ $8 \times 8 = \ldots$

$9 \times 9 = \ldots$ $10 \times 10 = \ldots$ $11 \times 11 = \ldots$ $12 \times 12 = \ldots$

Square numbers can also be written with a *little floating 2* just above a number's right shoulder. So 7x7 can also be written as 7^2. And $5^2 = 5 \times 5$.

So **8^2** is **8 squared**, which means **8x8**, which equals 64. Therefore, **$8^2 = 64$**.

2] Answer: **a)** $5^2 = \ldots$ **b)** $9^2 = \ldots$ **c)** $3^2 = \ldots$ **d)** $11^2 = \ldots$

A **cube number** is a number multiplied by itself, multiplied by itself *again*. So you times it by itself *twice*.

   $2 \times 2 \times 2 = 8$ $3 \times 3 \times 3 = 27$ $4 \times 4 \times 4 = 64$ $5 \times 5 \times 5 = 125$ *etc.*

Cube numbers can be written with a little floating 3: **2^3 = 2 cubed = 2x2x2 = 8**

3] Answer: **a)** $3^3 = \ldots$ **b)** $\ldots^3 = 125$ **c)** Trace the following $4^3, 6^3$

Check your answers on page 60, then add **1 point** to your full strength.

MULTIPLES

Multiples are like your multiplication tables (times tables). For instance, the **multiples of 3** are the numbers in the **3 times table**. It really is that simple. So the first ten multiples of 3 are: *3, 6, 9, 12, 15, 18, 21, 24, 27, 30*

1] a) Write the first ten **multiples of 5**: . . . .

b) Write the first ten **multiples of 7**: . . . .

c) Write the first ten **multiples of 8**: . . . .

Some multiples are easy to spot:
Multiples of 2 all end in <u>0</u> or an <u>even number</u>.
Multiples of 5 all end in <u>0</u> or <u>5</u>.
Multiples of 10 all end in <u>0</u>.

So **746** is a multiple of 2, as it ends in an even number.
   965 is a multiple of 5, as it ends in a 5.
   220 is a multiple of 2, 5 and 10, as it ends in a 0.

2] Answer the following, as in example **a)** below.

   a) 72 is a multiple of **2** (it's <u>even</u>), and also **8** and **9**, because 8x9 = 72.
   b) 35 is a multiple of ___(it ends in 5) and _____, because ___x5 = 35.
   c) 24 is a multiple of___(it's <u>even</u>), and ___ and ___ (choose two).

Finding **common multiples** is more tricky. If a number is a multiple of two different numbers, it is a common multiple. For instance, a common multiple of <u>3</u> and <u>4</u> is **12**, because 12 is a multiple of 3 **and** a multiple of 4. A common multiple of <u>4</u> and <u>8</u> is **16**, because 16 is a multiple of 4 **and** a multiple of 8.

To find a common multiple, first write out the times tables. Then simply look for a number that is in both lists.

<u>Find a common multiple of 6 and 8.</u>

6 times table: 6   12   18   24   30   36   42   48   54   60
8 times table: 8   16   24   32   40   48   56   64   72   80

As you can see, there are a couple to choose from here – **24** or **48**. In fact, there are an *infinite* amount, because the times tables go on forever. But we don't need that many.

3] <u>Find a common multiple of **6** and **9**</u>. First, write out the times tables, then circle a number that appears in both lists. That is your answer.

6 times table:

9 times table:

A multiple of 6 and 9 is . . . . .

Check your answers on page 60. Add **1 point** to your full speed and replenish your attributes. Then you have a choice. You can either carry on with the story (go to page 61) or if you wish you may complete the extra exercises for an extra reward (go to page 60).

1] (list of square numbers from 1^2 to 12^2)

  1   4   9   16   25   36   49   64   81   100   121   144

2] a) $5^2 = 25$ **b)** $9^2 = 81$ **c)** $3^2 = 9$ **d)** $11^2 = 121$

3] a) $3^3 = 27$ **b)** $5^3 = 125$ **c)** How was your tracing?

MUTLIPLES: Answers

1] a) Write the first ten **multiples of 5**:   5, 10, 15, 20, 25, 30, 35, 40, 45, 50

b) Write the first ten **multiples of 7**:   7, 14, 21, 28, 35, 42, 49, 56, 63, 70

c) Write the first ten **multiples of 8**:   8, 16, 24, 32, 40, 48, 56, 64, 72, 80

2] a) 72 is a multiple of **2** (it's <u>even</u>), and also **8** and **9**, because 8x9 = 72.

  b) 35 is a multiple of **5** (it ends in 5) and **7**, because 7x5 = 35.

  c) 24 is a multiple of **2** (it's <u>even</u>), and **4** & **6**, or **2** & **12**, or **3** & **8**.

3] <u>Find a common multiple of **6** and **9**.</u>

6 times table:	6	12	18	24	30	36	42	48	54	60	66	72
9 times table:	9	18	27	36	45	54	63	72	81	90	99	108

A multiple of 6 and 9 is **18** or **36** or **54** or **72**. (you only need one!)

EXTRA EXERCISES

First, cover the answers, which are at the bottom of the page!

1] Answer the following:

a) $6^2 =$ ____   **b)** $12^2 =$ ____   **c)** $3^3 =$ ____   **d)** $5^3 =$ ____

2] Find <u>one</u> common multiple of **8** and **12**.

Check your answers below, and add **1 point** to your full speed. Go to page 61.

EXTRA EXERCISES: Answers

1] a) 36   **b)** 144   **c)** 27   **d)** 125

2] **24** or **48** or **72** (or **96** of course, because 8x12 = 96)

CHAPTER EIGHT:
The Cell Block

"Drink again, and fill up your water skins in the rain," you say, as you follow your own advice. Then you head over to the raised portcullis and the ramp leading down into the gold mine.

I'm coming for you, Al'Nor, you think. *I'm coming for my staff.*

No guards rush out at you as you approach. They've seen and heard what you can do in the rain and want no part of it.

"Follow me." You head down the ramp, down and down, round and round.

You see the gate to the little chamber where you got jumped by the three guards earlier. The gate is ajar, as you left it, with the padlock on the floor. The bodies of the three guards, however, have been moved.

As you get nearer the gate you hold up a hand. *Stop. I'm not getting jumped again.*

You can't see or hear anyone beyond in the little chamber. But you have a feeling they're there, pressed up against the walls, out of sight, waiting for you to enter.

You slowly reach out a hand, grab one of the gate's iron bars and yank it shut. It *clangs* loudly. And sure enough, a knight appears, swinging his sword with a yell, and the blade crashes against the bars and rings like a bell, and the other prisoners jump, startled. You, however, are not startled. You kick the gate and it springs open, knocking the knight over, as you step into the chamber.

There are two others, one on either side, and the guy on the floor.

Knight		Knight		Knight	
Stre 10	Spd 7	Stre 10	Spd 4	Stre 11	Spd 7

The one in the middle has a lower speed because he's on his back. The other two are pretty quick, but you are quicker (aren't you always?), so can get in the first attack. You don't have time to use any magic, though. If you are defeated, return to Checkpoint 2 and complete the extra exercises on the page 60.

It is over, eventually. Mace against sword, against armour, against flesh. You hand your mace over to another prisoner and take one of the knights' swords. It is a better weapon. **Add 1 point to your full strength**.

It is now time to heal yourself. Complete the test below as normal, in 90 seconds, on a scrap piece of paper covering the answers. If you get 18 or more your strength completely replenishes. 16 or more, and it replenishes *mostly* – two points off full.

The Nine Times Table

1x9=9	2x9=18	3x9=27	4x9=36	5x9=45	6x9=54
7x9=63	8x9=72	9x9=81	10x9=90	11x9=99	12x9=108

THE TEST

1)5x9=	2)9x9=	3)2x9=	4)7x9=	5)8x9=
6)3x9=	7)12x9=	8)11x9=	9)6x9=	10)5x9=
11)1x9=	12)8x9=	13)3x9=	14)12x9=	15)4x9=
16)10x9=	17)2x9=	18)6x9=	19)9x9=	20)12x9=

ANSWERS

1) 45	2) 81	3) 18	4) 63	5) 72	6) 27	7) 108
8) 99	9) 54	10) 45	11) 9	12) 72	13) 27	14)108
15) 36	16) 90	17) 18	18) 54	19) 81	20) 108	

I hope you're feeling confident with your times tables.

You head down the staircase, passing the mine shafts as you go, expecting more knights to be waiting for you. But you make it to the bottom without incident.

And you gather around the metal door to the cell block, and you insert the key and turn it. The mechanism clicks. You push the door slowly open.

There are lots of guards in the cell block.

They hadn't expected you to be making an appearance – hadn't expected you to be able to open the door – and they turn round dumbly, a bit star struck. Clubmen, and macemen, and knights, in a crescent moon shape on the cell block floor.

The rest of the prisoners are still in their cells.

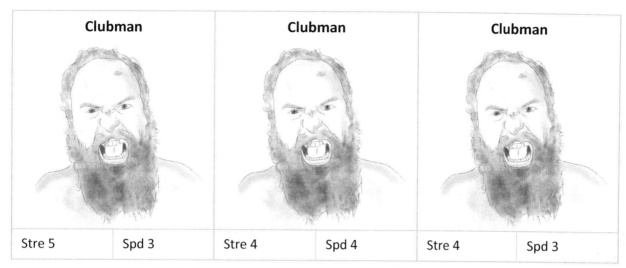

Clubman	Clubman	Clubman
Stre 5 · Spd 3	Stre 4 · Spd 4	Stre 4 · Spd 3

Knight	Knight	Knight
Stre 12 · Spd 8	Stre 15 · Spd 7	Stre 14 · Spd 8

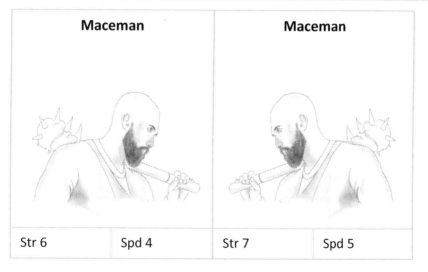

Maceman	Maceman
Str 6 · Spd 4	Str 7 · Spd 5

Now would probably be a good time to cast ARROW RAIN, don't you think? You only recently healed yourself, so your magic is still active, and I won't make you complete another test. Remember, it takes 6 hit points off *every enemy* in the battle. Cross out your water skin under your items. You've used it! Then play out the rest of the battle. You are faster than all of them, so after casting Arrow Rain you then get to attack someone first as well. If you fall, return to Checkpoint 2 on page 57.

The other prisoners have been watching through the bars in their cages. Most of them are shocked numb, but some start whooping and hollering, and you definitely hear the word *magic* thrown around quite a lot.

Then you notice the turnkey cowering in one of the corners, completely weapon-less. "P-please..." he mumbles. "All I do is open and close the cages..."

"Open them now."

"I c-can't... the master overrode the m-mechanism. You'll have to release each cage m-manually."

"And how do we do that?"

The turnkey swallows. "If I tell you, will you let me go?"

You shrug. "Okay. Yes."

He doesn't really have a choice, does he. He tells you the process for unlocking the cells. "N-now... will you let me go?"

You decide.

◦ If you keep your word and let him run, you gain one reputation point.

◦ If you go back on your word, you lose one reputation point, but you find a gold key after searching his body. Write *turnkey's key* in your items. That may come in useful. It may not. Who knows?

You have another choice. If you wish, you can pick up a second sword off one of the downed knights by the entrance. Having two swords will add 1 point to your strength, but take one point *off* your speed. So you'll be stronger but slower. If you do decide to pick it up, write *"2ⁿᵈ sword (+1 strength, -1 speed)"* under **items**, just to remind yourself you got it. You can drop this 2ⁿᵈ sword at any time, including mid-battle, thus losing that extra strength point, but regaining the 1 speed point you lost.

Worksheet Topic 5

ADDITION AND SUBTRACTION

The turnkey told you that the code for each cell involves either **adding** or **subtracting** the names (which are numbers) of all the prisoners in that cell.

There are three cells requiring addition and three cells requiring subtraction. We will open the *addition* cells first.

We will use *column addition*. Stack the numbers to be added, making sure you line up their place values (**Ones** over **Ones**, **Tens** over **Tens** *etc.*) And remember to carry the 1 whenever you need to!

Eg. Answer 4329 + 958.

STEP ONE:

Th	H	T	O
4	3	2	9
+	9	5	8
			7
		1	

Add the Ones:

9+8 = 17

So carry the 1!

STEP TWO:

Th	H	T	O
4	3	2	9
+	9	5	8
		8	7
		1	

Add the Tens, including the carried 1:

2+5+1 = 8

STEP THREE:

Th	H	T	O
4	3	2	9
+	9	5	8
5	2	8	7
1		1	

Repeat with the Hundreds and Thousands columns. Remember to carry the 1 whenever a column adds up to 10 or more.

You ask the prisoners in each cell what their numbers are. Luckily there aren't that many left! The answer to **c)** is the answer to **a)** plus the answer to **b)**.

1] Answer the following:

a) 734 + 290 =

Th	H	T	O
+			

b) 2107 + 1080 =

Th	H	T	O
+			

c) answer a + answer b =

Th	H	T	O
+			

2] Answer the following:

a) 1045 + 627 =

+

b) 3791 + 3980 =

+

c) answer a + answer b =

+

3] Answer the following. These require an extra column: the Ten Thousands column. Line the numbers up and carry the 1s exactly as before.

a) 7802 + 3030 =   **b)** 10 372 + 38 026 =   **c)** answer a + answer b =

+ _____   + _____   + _____
  _____   _____   _____

Now check your answers on page 68 and add **1 point** to your full strength.

SUBTRACTION

In subtraction, stack the numbers as before, lining up their place values. You will need to <u>exchange</u> whenever the top number is smaller than the bottom.

Eg. Answer 5248 + 2845.

STEP ONE:

Th	H	T	O	Subtract the
5	2	4	8	Ones:
- 2	8	4	5	**8-5 = 3**
			3	No problemo.

STEP TWO:

Th	H	T	O	Subtract the
5	2	4	8	Tens:
- 2	8	4	5	**4-4 = 0**
		0	3	Easy Peasy.

STEP THREE:

Th	H	T	O
^{4}5	^{1}2	4	8
- 2	8	4	5
	4	0	3

You can't do 2 minus 8, so you <u>exchange</u>. Take one from the column to the left, making the **5** a **4** and the **2** a **12**. Then:

12-8 = 4

STEP FOUR:

Th	H	T	O	Lastly,
^{4}5	^{1}2	4	8	**4-2 = 2.**
- 2	8	4	5	Done!
2	4	0	3	

1] Answer the following:

a) 1392 - 851 =   **b)** 6172 - 4056 =   **c)** 8462 – 3857 =

Th	H	T	O

Th	H	T	O

Th	H	T	O

Subtracting from a number with zeros is more difficult, because you have to exchange <u>twice</u>. Let's answer **502-345**.

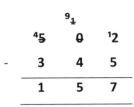

You can't do 2 minus 5, so you need to exchange… BUT there's a **0** in the Tens column! You therefore need to exchange from the Hundreds column *first*. Take one from the **5** (leaving 4 Hundreds) and give it to the Tens column, making that **0** a **10**. That's the first exchange. Now you can take 1 from that 10 (leaving 9 Tens) and give it to the Ones column, making 12 Ones. You can then complete the subtraction! **12-5 = 7**. And **9-4 = 5**. And lastly **4-3 = 1**.

2] Answer the following:

a) 5054 - 2836 =

b) 1047 - 965 =

c) 3204 – 1078 =

Check your answers on page 68, add **1 point** to your full speed and replenish your attributes. Now you can either continue with the story (go to page 69) or complete the extra exercises below for an extra reward.

EXTRA EXERCISES

TIP: Align the decimal points!

1] Add together:

a) 10 432 + 27 839

b) 238.92 + 79.30

c) 67.003 + 8.09

2] Subtract:

a) 56 024 – 31 855

b) 362.7 – 289.9

c) 12.29 – 7.3

Mark your answers on page 68. Add **1 point** to you full strength **and** full speed, replenish your attributes, then continue with the story on page 69.

ADDITION: Answers

1] a) 734 + 290 = **1024**   **b)** 2107 + 1080 = **3187**   **c)** 1024 + 3187 = **4211**

2] a) 1045 + 627 = **1672**   **b)** 3791 + 3980 = **7771**   **c)** 1672 + 7771 = **9443**

3] a) 7802 + 3030 = **10 832**   **b)** 10 372 + 38 026 = **48 398**   **c)** 10 832 + 48 398 = **59230**

SUBTRACTION: Answers

1] a) 1392-851 = **541**   **b)** 6172-4056 = **2116**   **c)** 8462–3857 = **4605**

2] a) 5054-2836 = **2218**   **b)** 1047-965 = **82**   **c)** 3204–1078 = **2126**

EXTRA EXERCISES: Answers

1] a) 10 432+27 839 = **38 271**   **b)** 238.92+79.30 = **318.22**   **c)** 67.003+8.09 = **75.093**

2] a) 56 024 – 31 855 = **24 169**   **b)** 362.7 – 289.9 = **72.8**   **c)** 12.29 – 7.3 = **4.99**

CHAPTER NINE:
Freedom Isn't Free

The last cage clanks open. Most of the freed prisoners have gathered in the wide gangways outside their cages. They are hungry. Weak. Exhausted. Weapon-less. Many are old. In fact, you estimate more than half will need help getting up the stairs. There are perhaps just a dozen young and strong in total. No doubt these men and women would in the near future have been sent to work down The Pit.

There are three who haven't been able to walk out of their cells. They are alive, but too sick or weak (or both) to move.

And you realise these prisoners, the ones you have come back for... they're not *strong enough* to escape.

Dammit.

Gord looks at you, and his expression says he's thinking the same thing. "They need medicine," he whispers. "They need food and water."

It was never just as simple as breaking them free and letting them run off into the mountains, waving their arms and cheering. You should have seen this coming.

"I am Aquaan," you say. "You probably noticed my magic. I'm an Elemental."

"You were a *prisoner* here," says one of the older ones you shared a cell with.

You tell them all about how for a year, ever since being underground, you've been unable to use your power. You needed the rain to reawaken it. "Luckily, it was raining on the way to The Pit."

"What are they doing down there?"

"I don't know. We didn't get that far."

"Well what are we going to do now?"

"Escape," says one of the younger ones. "Let's get the hell out of here."

"Easy for you to say. You're not sixty-three years old, with a bad hip."

"Or a bad back."

"Or arthritis."

"Or irritable bowel syndrome."

"Look at Seven Eighty," and the old woman points back into the cell she had once occupied, where an aging man lies flat on his back, struggling to breathe. "He's got the fever." She points to the cell across the gangway. "Look at the wound on his leg. It's infected. He'll probably lose it in a few days."

The man with the badly gashed leg says, "I had an accident with a pickaxe. Wait, what?"

"And none of us have weapons," the old woman continues, and then waggles a finger at you and your ragtag band. "Except you lot. How are we going to defend ourselves from the mountain wolves, if we get out? Or when the guards come, because we all know they will. And I know what kind of things they got in the armoury, let me tell you. They put me to work in there, cleaning and sharpening the weapons. Well, not going to be much use digging, am I?"

"What's your name?" you ask.

"One One Five."

"No, your *real* name."

"Oh. Lilleth. At least, I think it was."

"Okay, Lilleth. I'll go to the armoury. Get some weapons for those who want them. And some armour for everyone else. Even lightweight leathers will give you some protection. And I'll go to the healing bay too. Get some bandages, goatweed, finberry roots." You unfurl the map of the mine. "Actually, the armoury and healing bay aren't far at all."

"No," says Lilleth. "They're both just out that door." She points to the gate in the far wall. "Down a long corridor."

A few of the others look over your shoulder at the map.

Twenty-Three is still the tallest out of everyone. He traces his finger along the map, from the barracks up to Al'Nor's residence, and then follows the path left to the gatehouse hut in the courtyard. "The guards can go through Al'Nor's house, round the courtyard, back into the mines through the main gate and come at us through that door." And he points to the main door you'd unlocked and come through.

"Let's close it for now. And lock it."

"I'm sure they'll be able to unlock it, Aquaan."

"We'll leave the key in the keyhole," you say. "That might stop them from getting in."

Twenty-Three thinks about it. "Maybe."

Gord says, "It might work."

You go over and shut that door, lock it and leave the key in. "Okay. So I need to go through *that* one." And you point at the opposite gate. "The one Al'Nor always comes and goes through with his men."

"Yes."

"Right." You address your ragtag band. "You need to stay here, just in case the guards get in. Defend the rest of the prisoners." Then you raise your voice to the entire cell block. "I need water. As much of it as you can spare. I can't use my powers without it, and I have a feeling I'm going to need them."

If your reputation is 13 or higher, the freed prisoners donate to you as much water as they can find, filling three water skins – that's three spells. Add them to your item list now. If your reputation is 12 or lower, the freed prisoners are less giving, and only fill two waters skins – that's enough for two spells. Add them to your item list now.

"Be careful," Gord says.

"I will. Hand out the rest of the weapons from those guards by the door. There are some clubs, maces, a couple of swords, I think." You head down the gangway, through the crowd, which parts for you. The expressions on their faces are a mixture of awe, fear, wonder and gratitude.

Now to open the gate in the far wall.

There's a stone pressure pad built into the wall next to the gate, with an inscription carved above it.

I will open when I'm in my prime

Mmm. What a strange little cryptic clue. The pressure pad looks like this:

1	2	3	4
5	6	7	8
9	10	11	12
13	14	15	16

The numbers run from 1-16. It sounds awfully like you need to push in the **prime numbers**, doesn't it? Well, what are prime numbers, and how do we work them out?

Firstly, we need to look at **factors**. A factor is a whole number that divides exactly into a certain number. For instance, the <u>factors of 12</u> are **1, 2, 3, 4, 6** and **12**. Factors come in <u>pairs</u>. In this instance: **1** and **12** (because 1x12=12), **2** and **6** (because 2x6=12), and **3** and **4** (3x4=12).

When working out the factors of a number, go through methodically, starting from 1 (which will *always* be a factor), using your times tables.

For example: list the factor pairs of **18**.

1x**18** = 18
2x**9** = 18
3x**6** = 18
4x nothing = 18, so 4 IS NOT a factor
5x nothing = 18, so 5 IS NOT a factor
6x**3** = 18, but we've already found out that 3 and 6 are factors, so here we <u>stop</u>.

1] First, <u>cover the answers at the top of page 73</u>! Now, list the factor pairs of:

a) 15   **b) 10**   **c) 24**   **d) 13**

Now check your answers on page 73. Add **1 point** to your full strength.

What did you notice about the answer to **d)**? Yep. 13 only has *2* factors: 1 and itself. This means it is **PRIME**. Say with me:

"A prime number only has 2 factors: 1 and itself."

The number **1** doesn't count as prime (because it doesn't have two factors), but the number **2** *does*. **2 is the only EVEN prime number.**

3 and **5** are also prime. Then, all other prime numbers end in either **1, 3, 7** or **9**.

1	2	3	4
5	6	7	8
9	10	11	12
13	14	15	16

Look at the pressure pad. Circle the prime numbers **2, 3** and **5**. Now circle **13**, too, because we discovered that was prime in question **1]d)**.

The only other numbers on the pressure pad grid that might be prime (because they end in 1, 3, 7 or 9) are **7, 9** and **11**.

2] Which of these numbers (**7, 9** and **11**) are prime numbers? Then circle them on the pressure pad above.

Check your answer on page 73 and add **1 point** to your full will, making it 8. You know what that means. You now have enough will to cast **Vortex**! Vortex does **12** damage to **one** enemy in battle.

   You can now choose to continue with the story on page 74, or complete the extra exercises on page 73.

FACTORS AND PRIMES: Answers

1] a) **15:** 1 and 15, 3 and 5   b) **10:** 1 and 10, 2 and 5

   c) **24:** 1 and 24, 2 and 12, 3 and 8, 4 and 6   d) **13:** 1 and 13

2] **7** and **11** are prime (9 has the factor *3*, as well as 1 and itself, so it is not).

EXTRA EXERCISES

First, cover the answers at the bottom of the page!

1] Answer the following about *common factors*:

eg.) Underline the numbers that have **4** as a common factor (ie. Those numbers that are in the 4 times table).

9   <u>12</u>   23   18   <u>20</u>   <u>32</u>

a) Underline the numbers that have **3** as a common factor.

9   12   23   18   20   32

b) Underline the numbers that have **2** as a common factor.

9   12   23   18   20   32

c) Underline the **prime** number.

9   12   23   18   20   32

Now check your answers below, add **1 point** to your full speed, replenish your attributes, and continue with the story on page 74.

continue with the story on page 74.

EXTRA EXERCISES: Answers

1]a)	<u>9</u>	<u>12</u>	23	<u>18</u>	20	32
b)	9	<u>12</u>	23	<u>18</u>	<u>20</u>	<u>32</u>
c)	9	12	<u>23</u>	18	20	32

CHAPTER TEN:
Blades And Plants

"Okay. Let's see if this works."

You push in the numbers on the pressure pad – 2, 3, 5, 7, 11, and finally 13 – and there's a *click* as you do so, and the gate trundles open.

Knight

Str 15	Spd 8

You are about to step into the corridor when there is a roar from beyond the threshold. It is a bit of a clue that someone is there, to be honest.

You step back as the knight appears in the open gateway and thrashes his sword against the stone, which is where you had been a moment before.

"You shouldn't have yelled," you say. "Bit of a weird one. Might as well have shouted *Watch Out!*"

He doesn't make conversation.

You don't have time to use your magic. If you fall, the last checkpoint is page 71.

You defeat yon yelling knight and he collapses in a sitting position against the corridor wall.

"Okay," you say. "I think it's clear. But shut the gate behind me."

"Where are you going first?" Gord asks. "The armoury, or the healing bay?"

◦ If you want to go to the armoury first, go to page 75.

◦ If you want to go to the healing bay first, go to page 84.

Weapons, you think. For yourself, and anyone who wants one. And armour for everyone else.

You head towards the armoury, sword out and pointed, keeping to the walls, slow and steady like your training taught you.

The corridor is basically straight, but it is pocked and uneven and gloomy. Plenty of places for the guards of Al'Nor to hide in wait – just for an opportunity like this.

You've been trying to see every nook and cranny, every cleft in the cave wall, but these guards found a good place to hide. Behind a stalagmite. Crouched in the shadows. Pressed into a crack. They all come at you at once, before you can use your magic.

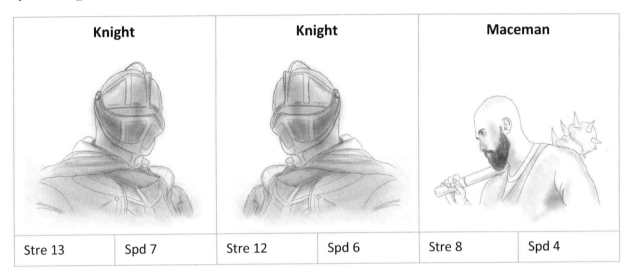

Knight		Knight		Maceman	
Stre 13	Spd 7	Stre 12	Spd 6	Stre 8	Spd 4

Sneak attack! The knight on the left gets in his attack before you react, and does you a little bit of damage. Then the sneak attack is over and you should compare speeds to see who attacks next. Spoiler: it's you. If you fall, return to checkpoint 3 on page 71.

You deal with the three enemies. Knight one is half way up the corridor. Knight two is lodged in a crack in the wall, back where he came from. And the maceman is lying in the remains of a stalagmite.

Complete this test in 90 seconds to heal yourself. If you get 18 or more, your strength replenishes completely. If you get 16 or more, your strength only replenishes *mostly* – 2 points off full. The answers are on page 76.

You only use a little water, so you don't need to cross off one of your water skins. You've still got them for battle magic.

THE TEST				
1)8x2=	2)3x1=	3)7x9=	4)6x11=	5)5x12=
6)4x6=	7)12x9=	8)6x8=	9)4x4=	10)7x4=
11)6x6=	12)8x3=	13)5x4=	14)12x4=	15)7x5=
16)10x11=	17)8x9=	18)6x4=	19)9x2=	20)3x7=

You get to the end of the corridor without having to face any more enemies. The armoury door is thick dull metal that rings when you hit it with the pommel of your sword.

Instead of a keyhole, the door has a column of metal latches connecting it to the door frame, making it look like a complicated metal insect. A series of sliders are attached to the frame-side of each latch.

Each slider has a row of numbers printed across it, and you move one of them with two fingers, back and forth, just to see how well it slides.

Beneath each slider, on the frame itself, is an embossed dot, which does *not* move with the slider. And you realise suddenly it acts as a decimal point.

Checkpoint 4

Worksheet Topic 7
MULTIPLYING & DIVIDING BY 10, 100 AND 1000

By moving the slider **left**, the digits move to the left and, because the decimal point stays in the same place, the number gets **bigger** by multiples of 10. By moving the slider to the **right**, the digits move right, and the number gets **smaller** by a multiple of 10.

The decimal point does NOT move. The digits move.

And it is NOT just as simple as adding a zero or two.

If you multiply by 10, you move the digits one place to the left, *keeping the decimal point in the same place*. If you multiply by 100, you move the digits two places. If you multiply by 1000, move three places. The number of zeros tells you how many places to move.

TIP: You can remember that multiply means move LEFT, because MULTIPLY has **L**s in it, and *divide* doesn't.

eg) 48.943 x 100 = **4894.3**   (the **digits** have moved **2** places to the **left**)

If the question involves a whole number (without a decimal point)... simply put the decimal point in yourself.

eg) 985 x 10 = 985.0 x 10 = **9850.**

1] Answer the following:

a) 37.8 x 10   **b)** 90 x 1000   **c)** 88.062 x 100   **d)** 0.72 x 1000

When you divide by a multiple of 10, the process is the same, except you move the digits to the **right** instead of the left.

eg) 73.72 ÷ 10 = **7.372**

2] Answer the following:

a) 71823 ÷ 1000   **b)** 36.2 ÷ 10   **c)** 0.06 ÷ 10   **d)** 23.7 ÷ 100

Check your answer on page 78. Add **2 points** to your full strength. Now choose to continue with the story on page 79, or complete the extra exercises below.

Check your answer on page 78. Now choose to continue with the story on page 79, or complete the extra exercises below.

EXTRA EXERCISES

1] a) 739.9 ÷ 100   **b)** 26 ÷ 1000   **c)** 47.002 x 100

d) 0.06 ÷ 10   **e)** 89.279 x 1000   **f)** 0.6 x 10

Now check your answers on page 78, and add **1 point** to your full speed. Continue with the story on page 79.

Now check your answers on page 78, and add **1 point** to your full speed. Continue with the story on page 79.

MULTIPLYING AND DIVIDING BY 10, 100 AND 1000: Answers

1] a) 37.8 x 10 = **378**　　　　**b)** 90 x 1000 = **90 000**

c) 88.062 x 100 = **8806.2**　　　**d)** 0.72 x 1000 = **720**

2] a) 71823 ÷ 1000 = **71.823**　　　**b)** 36.2 ÷ 10 = **3.62**

c) 0.06 ÷ 10 = **0.006**　　　**d)** 23.7 ÷ 100 = **0.237**

EXTRA EXERCISES: Answers

1] a) 739.9 ÷ 100 = **7.399**　　　**b)** 26 ÷ 1000 = **0.026**

c) 47.002 x 100 = **4700.2**　　　**d)** 0.06 ÷ 10 = **0.006**

e) 89.279 x 1000 = **89 279**　　　**f)** 0.6 x 10 = **6**

The locking mechanism clanks, and the column of latches pops open like a metal insect taking wing. You pull the door wide, hinges whining, revealing racks of weaponry, lined up along the walls and in aisles down the middle of the large room.

And then you hear loud thudding footsteps, and into view steps the biggest man you have ever seen.

Big guys make you laugh because of their little heads.

He looks past you, and his brows furrow – not that you can see much; he wears a heavy semi-spherical helmet like a Christmas pudding, with only small holes for his eyes.

"I heard there was a riot," he growls. "Where are the rest of you?"

"I don't need anyone else," you say.

He laughs, heaving into view a colossal broad sword. "Look at you. You look like you're wearing an old potato sack."

"You look like you're wearing a Christmas pudding on your head."

He doesn't like that. He doesn't understand it, but he doesn't like it. He lumbers up to the door, and you back up a few steps.

"Think I'll call you Sandra," you say. "Is that okay?"

"My name is The Blacksmith."

"The - Blacksmith? Like, your first name's *The*?"

You hear running footsteps behind you. Two knights slow to a jog as they approach.

"Oh hi. Have you met Sandra?"

The three of them stand in a triangle around you. The Blacksmith ducks his head and steps out of the armoury. "Stop calling me *Sandra*. That was my mother's name."

"You have to be kidding."

"You die now."

Take the following test to activate your magic. You have 90 seconds. If you get 18 or more, you can use a spell in the battle with the Blacksmith. The answers are at the top of the next page. And remember, you also get to attack first after you've cast your spell, because you're faster than your enemies.

THE TEST				
1)8x8=	2)3x6=	3)7x3=	4)11x11=	5)5x8=
6)8x6=	7)12x3=	8)6x6=	9)4x7=	10)9x4=
11)6x5=	12)8x4=	13)5x10=	14)11x4=	15)7x7=
16)8x11=	17)8x7=	18)6x12=	19)9x2=	20)3x8=

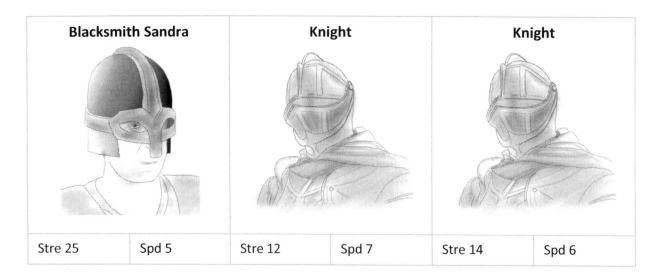

Blacksmith Sandra		Knight		Knight	
Stre 25	Spd 5	Stre 12	Spd 7	Stre 14	Spd 6

If you use a spell (and I recommend you do), remember to cross out one of your water skin items. If you fall, return to checkpoint 4 on page 76.

Sandra was a strong brute, but he was no match for an Elemental mage.

You head into the armoury and have a good look round at all the weapons and armour. There's a great range to choose from.

If you're currently holding two swords, discard one of them. Take one point off your strength and add one point to your speed. So you're currently browsing the weapons and armour with just your primary sword.

You may pick **one piece** of armour to wear.

ARMOUR

Chestplate and gauntlets: +1 strength
Heavy armour: +2 strength, -1 speed
Light chain mail: +1 speed

Adjust your character card accordingly. You can now also choose from the following weapon combinations.

You can choose to put down your current primary sword and pick up **one** of the following weapons, which require two hands:

Blacksmith's Broad Sword; Must be used two-handed: +3 strength, -1 speed

Long Sword; Must be used two-handed: +2 strength

Blacksmith's Broad Sword   Long Sword

Alternatively, you can keep your current primary sword and pick up with your free hand **one** of the following: a shield or a sabre.

Shield; Requires a free hand: +2 speed

Sabre; Can be used with one hand: +1 strength, + 1 speed

Shield   Sabre

Or, if you have the turnkey's key, you may open the locked safe in the corner. Inside you find a curved dagger, which you may also pick up for your free hand.

Curved Dagger; Can be used with one hand: +1 strength, +2 speed

Curved Dagger

There are a lot of options for you to choose from. Anyhow, you should be leaving with both hands occupied, either with two weapons, a two-handed weapon, or one weapon and a shield. If you've got a free hand, for heaven's sake go back in and pick something else up. Make sure you've updated your character card.

You then fill a wooden trolley with weapons and armour for the rest of the freed prisoners and head back to the cell block.

Everyone is happy to see you and what you've brought back. If your reputation is 11 or lower, add 1 point to it.

"Was the Blacksmith there?" asks Lilleth.

"You mean Sandra?"

"Sandra? I'm pretty sure that's not his name."

"He wasn't so tough. Head too small for his body."

To replenish your attributes, you must heal yourself with a little water. Again, you don't need to worry about crossing off any water skins; you don't need that much so can keep whatever you've got left (if anything) for your battle magic.

As normal, you have 90 seconds. You need 18 or more to replenish everything fully. 16 of more replenishes your speed, but your strength and will only replenish up to 2 points below its full score. Cover the answers at the bottom of the page!

THE TEST				
1)8x4=	2)3x8=	3)7x6=	4)6x2=	5)8x12=
6)4x7=	7)11x3=	8)6x3=	9)4x8=	10)5x4=
11)6x5=	12)8x4=	13)5x5=	14)10x11=	15)7x3=
16)12x9=	17)7x9=	18)9x4=	19)5x2=	20)8x7=

ANSWERS						
1) 32	2) 24	3) 42	4) 12	5) 96	6) 28	7) 33
8) 18	9) 32	10) 20	11) 30	12) 32	13) 25	14)110
15) 21	16) 108	17) 63	18) 36	19) 10	20) 56	

○ If you have already been to the healing bay, go to page 88.

○ If you still need to go to the healing bay, go there now. It's page 84.

You've returned alone to the old cave-in just off *the freezer*, intrigued with what lies beyond. And you summon vortex (cross out one water skin), and blast the blockage with your magic. A tremendous *crack* echoes around the shaft as rock and stone spirals aside. The shock brings more debris down from the ceiling, but this too is thrown away by your magic. Eventually you are left with a path through the tunnel.

Okay. What have we got?

You take a wall torch from its sconce and proceed forward, past the cave-in and into a shaft left alone for years. The air smells stale and heavy.

You see the first skeleton almost straight away. He or she (you have no way of knowing) must have been buried beneath the cave-in. A full water skin lies next to them, uncovered from its burial place. Add it to your items now.

You continue walking, and after only a minute or two you come across more skeletons, a group of them this time. Their clothes have not yet decayed, and you can tell the rags of the prisoners from the tough leather armour of the guards.

And then you come across the bones of the man who must have been the High Protector. His red surcoat is tattered rags, but the metal armour won't rot. In fact, the golden gauntlets and greaves are still shiny, and identical to the ones Caesar wears now. You take the gauntlets and slide them over your arms. They are a definite upgrade to what you wear now. Add 2 points to your full strength and 1 point to your full speed.

Now return to the page you were on previously, before you came here, and continue with your adventure.

People are sick, you think. You need medical supplies. You double check the map. "Okay everyone. I'll be back soon."

It doesn't take you too long to reach the short stub of corridor leading to the healing bay. The floor is ragged with fallen rocks and the walls are uneven and scarred like the gills of a fish. There are plenty of places to hide. Indeed, as soon as you start towards the healing bay's old iron gate, an archer appears from behind a column and looses an arrow at you. Your instincts kick in and you dive to the ground, the arrow whistling above your head, narrowly missing you.

Woah, that was close.

You scuttle behind a near stalagmite, as you hear another arrow *twang* and *thwip* by. That one must have come from a second archer; there hadn't been time for the first to nock and loose another arrow. You watch it imbed itself in the far wall and wobble there.

There follows a couple of moments of silence as you all wait for each other to make the next move.

"Do you mind telling me how many of you there are?" you ask.

You don't expect an answer, but then one of the archers yells back, *"A million!"*

Pants on fire. But there are at least two. Perhaps more. You saw where one of the archers was hiding - behind that column – and by looking at the direction of the second arrow, the one sticking out of the wall (and by the fact that arrows fly in a straight line), you can work out where the second archer is.

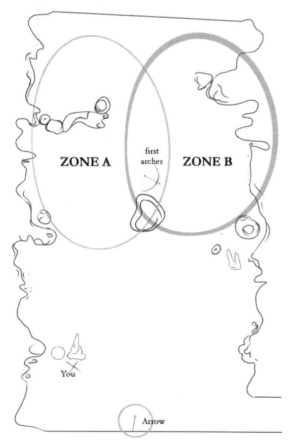

You can bring down the cave ceiling on anyone underneath with your spell *Vortex*. But only half the ceiling. At the moment this seems the most sensible plan. So which zone is the second archer in, **Zone A** or **Zone B**? Write your answer here ___. This is the area of the ceiling where you'll focus your magic.

You pop the lid off your water skin (go ahead and cross one water skin off from your items) and coax the water out with your magic. It rises out into the open in thick, glowing globules and begins to spin above the palm of your hand. Then you focus on the cave roof, the water spinning faster and faster into a vortex, and you cast it at the ceiling.

There is a tremendous *crack* as the spell rips the ceiling apart, throwing huge chunks of rock down on those below. The column where the first archer is hiding gets obliterated, reduced to grit and gravel. You jump up from your shelter as the dust plumes out through the corridor, and you run forward into the cloud. If you calculated correctly, you'll have worked out the second archer is in Zone B, and buried him along with the first. You make it to the end of the corridor, skirting round the fallen debris, and there are no more enemies waiting for you.

If you incorrectly blasted Zone A, you run through the dust cloud, only to find the second archer waiting for you at the end. He was shaken by the explosion, but unhurt, and he's recovered his senses quick enough to raise his bow. When you appear through the smog he shoots an arrow straight into your thigh.

You scream and tumble to your knees at his feet as he fumbles for another arrow. This time he's too slow, and you defeat him with a roar of anger and pain. You manage to pull out the arrow and heal yourself, but you'll have a little stiffness in that leg for a while. So at the start of the <u>next two</u> battles you must subtract 1 point from your full speed. After those two battles your leg returns to normal and you can start at full speed.

For now, completely replenish your strength, speed and will.

You turn your attention on the healing bay's old iron gate, kicking aside chunks of the ceiling.

Worksheet Topic 8
LONG MULTIPLICATION

One of the archers has a piece of paper claiming that the code to open the healing bay's gate can be worked out using long multiplication. Bit weird, isn't it, but there we go. You need to be able to multiply a four-digit number by a two-digit number. You need to use your times tables and column addition.

Eg. What is **6381 x 48**?

First we do **6381 x 8**, then **6381 x 40**, and then add the answers together. Turn over to see step-by-step working.

STEP ONE:

```
      Th  H  T  O
          6  3  8  1
  X             4  8
  ─────────────────────
  5   1  0  4  8
          3  6
  ─────────────────────
```

Multiply the **8** of **48** by each digit of the top number, right to left:

8x1 = 8 | 8x8 = 64
8x3 = 24 | 8x6 = 48

Make sure you add the carried numbers! 24 add the carried 6 is **30**. 48 add the carried 3 is **51**.

STEP TWO:

```
      Th  H  T  O
          6  3  8  1
  X             4  8
  ─────────────────────
  5   1  0  4  8
                   0
  ─────────────────────
```

Put a **0** in the right corner of the 2nd line, as we will now be multiplying by Tens, not Ones.

STEP THREE:

```
        Th  H  T  O
            6  3  8  1
    X             4  8
    ─────────────────────
      5   1  0  4  8
  2   5   5  2  4  0
            1  3
    ─────────────────────
```

Multiply the **4** of **48** by each digit of the top number.

4x1 = 4 | 4x8 = 32
4x3 = 12 | 4x6 = 24

Again, remember to add the carried numbers. 12 add the carried 3 is **15**. 24 add the carried 1 is **25**.

STEP FOUR:

```
        Th  H  T  O
            6  3  8  1
    X             4  8
    ─────────────────────
      5   1  0  4  8
  2   5   5  2  4  0
  ─────────────────────
  3   0   6  2  8  8
  1
```

Lastly, add the columns!

First cover the answers at the bottom of the page! Then answer the following questions in the book below, using the same steps as the example.

1] Work out 3652 x 29

```
      Th   H   T   O
           3   6   5   2
  X               2   9
  ─────────────────────

                       0
  ─────────────────────

  ─────────────────────
```

2] Work out 4802 x 72

```
      Th   H   T   O
           4   8   0   2
  X               7   2
  ─────────────────────

  ─────────────────────

  ─────────────────────
```

Check your answers. Add **1 point** to both your full strength and full speed.

MULTIPLICATION: Answers

1] 3652 x 29 = 105 908   **2]** 4802 x 72 = 345 744

The gate rises, and you head into the healing bay. There are rolls of bandages, pulped goatweed for making antiseptic poultices for open wounds, and finberry roots, which have antibiotic properties when eaten.

You now have a new **healing** ability. Both finberry roots and goatweed poultices can be used *mid-battle*. Finberry roots add 5 points to your strength (up to your full strength score – not above it!) and you can chew them whilst attacking. This means that during your turn, you can use a finberry root <u>*and then still attack*</u> as well. A goatweed poultice takes longer to apply, and you need your hands to do so. This means that you use it *as your turn*. You cannot then attack as well. However, goatweed completely replenishes your strength.

You can also, of course, use these plants at any time outside of battle for the same effect.

As you know, you cannot use spells mid-battle, whether that be Arrow Rain or Vortex, or healing magic, because you don't have the time. Now you can use these plants if you need to.

You are able to carry 3 healing items on your person at one time. Choose from the goatweed and finberry roots. You may carry all three of one plant, or two of one plant and one of the other. It's up to you. Write them down in your items.

If you want to write "*+5*" next to finberry roots and "*full strength, 1 turn*" next to goatweed, or something similar so you don't forget, that's up to you.

Okay, you're all set. You untie your cloak and fill it with healing items for the freed prisoners and drag it back to the cell room. There you let your cloak fall open and pass round the extra medical supplies (don't worry, the three plants you've chosen for yourself you keep, and no one begrudges you that).

If your reputation is 11 or lower, you gain one reputation point.

◦ If you have already been to the armoury, go to page 88.

◦ If you still need to go to the armoury, go there now. It's page 75.

CHAPTER ELEVEN:
Food And Water

Both the armoury and healing bay plundered, and the bounty lies piled in the middle of the cell block floor.

"Any incidents?" you ask Gord.

"No, not really. Anyone try to get through the main door?" And you point to the other end of the room at the bulky metal door you left the key in.

"No, I don't think so."

"That's good. We better do something with all this kit, then, hadn't we."

It's time to divide the armour, weapons and medical supplies around the group.

Worksheet Topic 9

SHORT DIVISION

This method is best when you're dividing by a one-digit number. In theory, you should be able to use it when dividing by either 11 or 12, too, because you know your 11 and 12 times tables.

Eg. Answer 3648÷6

STEP ONE: First, set out the equation like this:
Starting from the **left** (unlike multiplication, which starts from the right) try to divide each digit of the big number digit by 6.

$$6 \,|\, 3 \quad 6 \quad 4 \quad 8$$

STEP TWO: 3 doesn't divide by 6... but **36** does!

$$\begin{array}{c} \quad\; 6 \\ 6 \,|\, 3 \; 6 \; 4 \; 8 \end{array}$$

STEP THREE: 4 doesn't divide by 6, so put in a 0.

$$\begin{array}{c} \quad\; 6 \; 0 \\ 6 \,|\, 3 \; 6 \; 4 \; 8 \end{array}$$

STEP FOUR: 48 *does* divide by 6 – by 8!

$$\begin{array}{c} \quad\; 6 \; 0 \; 8 \\ 6 \,|\, 3 \; 6 \; 4 \; 8 \end{array}$$

So 3648÷6 = **608**.

1] Answer the following in the book:

a) 3284÷4

b) 1463÷7

c) 5155÷5

$$4\overline{)3\quad2\quad8\quad4}$$

$$7\overline{)1\quad4\quad6\quad3}$$

$$5\overline{)5\quad1\quad5\quad5}$$

Sometimes a number won't divide perfectly by another, and there is a *remainder* left over. For example: 12 prisoners want a weapon, and there are 17 weapons available. **17÷12** is **1 with remainder 5**. This means that everyone who wants a weapon gets a weapon, and there are 5 weapons left over.

2] There are **8** young men and women strong enough to wear heavy armour. In total there are **43** separate pieces: metal helmets, shields, chest plates, metal gauntlets and greaves. How many separate pieces can the 8 young prisoners each have, and what is remaining?

3] For the remaining **12** prisoners, there is a mixture of lighter leather helmets and body armour, some chain mail, and hundreds of smaller leather wraps for arms, legs, hands and feet. In total, there are **247** pieces of light armour. How many separate pieces can the 12 remaining prisoners each have, and what is remaining?

4] There are **20** prisoners in total. There are **68** medical items. How many medical items does each prisoner get, and what's the remainder?

Check your answers on page 90. Add **1 point** to your strength, then continue with the story.

1] a) 3284÷4 = **821**   **b)** 1463÷7 = **209**   **c)** 5155÷5 = **1031**

2] 43÷8 = **5 remainder 3**

3] 247÷12 = **20 remainder 7**

4] 68÷20 = **3 remainder 8**

"There's another problem," Gord says, as the injured and sick are being seen to, and everyone else is kitting themselves out with armour, or weapons, or both.

"Go on."

"We don't have any food."

"Right."

"And hardly any water. We've given most of it to you."

"Mmm. I did need it," you say, and Gord shakes his head.

"I'm not saying you didn't. But we don't know how long it'll be until we reach civilisation. We can't go without food and water. The rain won't last."

"I know."

"There's the food store and well on the map you've got. I noticed earlier."

"I noticed too." You get out and unfurl the map. "There." You point.

"Right next to the barracks."

You sigh. "Of course."

Right under Al'Nor's house.

At that moment, a *boooom* echoes from outside the cell block, *through* the cell block, shaking the room, rattling dust from the ceiling. The freed prisoners duck their heads and cry out in surprise.

"What the hell was that?" Gord asks, shoulders still hunched.

You're all looking at the gate, the one you left through to the armoury and healing bay. The one leading to the food store and well, and the barracks, and Al'Nor.

"Sounded like a cave-in," someone says, as a dust cloud begins wafting through the gate from further along the mines.

"Not a cave-in," you say. "It was an explosion."

"An *explosion*?"

"They've blown one of the corridors, brought the roof down. On purpose."

"They're trying to block us in?"

"No." You bite your lip. "They're trying to block us out. Stop us coming any further." You watch the dust cloud creep in and then settle like a shroud.

"They're scared of us!" says one of the men, and starts laughing.

"They're not scared of you, Three Two Eight, you big ninny. They're scared of *Aquaan*."

Which is undoubtedly true. You don't take any notice of the comment. You stand in the open gateway and look in the direction of the cave-in.

Gord appears at your side. "What happens if they try to block the other side of the cell block, too. If they blow up the stairs leading to the courtyard we'll be stuck down here."

"I know."

"But we can't leave yet – we don't have any food or water..."

You purse your lips. "I have a nasty feeling they might have just blocked our way to the well and food store. Blocked the corridor. We might not be able to get to them after all."

Gord curses. "Well, I guess we can only go and see."

You nod. "Yes. Come with me to the cave-in? We'll inspect it and make a decision. See whether we can get through or not. Decide whether we stay or whether we go."

"Okay."

You tell the rest of the freed prisoners what's happening and then you and Gord head towards the blockage. Dust still hangs in the air, and the floor is white with the stuff, and you leave footprints behind as if you're walking through a fine snow.

Further along the torches have gutted out, smothered by the dust, or blown out by the wind from the explosion. You and Gord pick up the last two still flaming and carry them on, deeper into the darkness.

"So what's your story?" Gord asks eventually.

You look at him. "What do you mean?"

"You're an Elemental. Where do you come from? Why are you here?"

You chuckle. "I'm here because Al'Nor captured me, when I'd lost my powers. I had no water and I'd lost my staff, so I had no magic."

"I know, you told me that. I mean, why are the Eleven of you here? Where did you come from?"

"We're here because the monsters are here."

"And how are the monsters here? Where did *they* come from?"

You sigh, wondering how much to say. "They came from the ground. From *under* the ground."

"From underground? Great. Like... from where we are now, then."

"This is a *mine*, Gord. We're here because people were digging for gold, not because there are monsters living here." Although Al'Nor is his own kind of monster, you suppose.

"And where did you come from? You Eleven?"

"What do you mean?"

"Well, if you Eleven Elementals existed before the monsters came you kept it very quiet, didn't you. We start hearing rumours of monsters a few years back, and then we hear rumours about magical people fighting them."

"It's... complicated," you say. *And classified.*

"Are you even human?"

You raise your eyebrows at him. "Oh, thanks."

"I'm just asking. What's happened... it's crazy. It doesn't make sense."

"I know. I've been here nearly a year, remember. It's been a year since I last spoke to the Eleven. That was when they sent me after Drojinn..."

"Drojinn?"

"Drojinn. The flying snake monster thing I was fighting over the mountains. It's name is Drojinn."

"It has a name?"

"Of course it has a name. And we didn't know it could fly, or we would have sent one of the other Eleven. Probably Mistra. She can fly too."

"Right..."

"And things were getting bad. Most of the monsters were coming out of the South Pole, and no one lived there. But they were moving north. The Eleven of us could deal with them... but more kept coming. Too many. We couldn't hold them back, and they were reaching the southern-most Kingdoms. Angowa. Lore."

"Here," Gord added. "Sha'Pan."

"And it's been nearly a year. I dread to think what Numera's like out there now."

"Well hopefully we'll be able to find out soon."

The floor now is thick with dust, and the mine walls are scarred and pockmarked. Finally, the two of you reach the cave-in. The corridor is plugged in solid black rock that's still warm to the touch. You strike it with your weapon and it rings and echoes.

"Can you use your magic to get through?" Gord asks.

But you sigh. "No. Unfortunately not."

"There's a crack there, at the bottom." Gord crouches, bringing his torch to the lowest corner of the blockage.

"I might be able to squeeze through," you say. "Mind out."

You lie on your belly and push your weapon through first, to help clear any stray debris, and to feel the way. "I don't really want to bring my torch," you say. "It's too tight. I'll burn my face off."

"Shame your magic doesn't include shining light out of your palms."

"Funnily enough, one of the Eleven *can* do that. But not me. Hold the torch low?" You slither forward into the crack, trying to work out whether you can carry on or not.

Worksheet Topic 10
THOUSANDTHS

One thousandth can be written as $\dfrac{1}{1000}$ (a fraction) or **0.001** (a decimal).

Decimals have place values, just like whole numbers. They are called **Tenths, Hundredths, Thousandths** etc.

Ones	Tenths	Hund-redths	Thous-andths
2 .	4	9	6

The number **2.496** is very close to 2.5, which is two and a half.

1] a) Write **5 hundredths** as a **decimal**.

b) Write **9 thousandths** as a **fraction**.

c) In the number **0.3741**, how many **thousandths** are there?

Now, back to you crawling through the collapsed tunnel.

2] On your belly, you are **14.742cm** high and **56.723cm** wide. But your armour adds **1.544cm** to your height and **1.893cm** to your width.

   a) Work out your total height.
   b) Work out your total width.

3] The tunnel shrinks the further you go in. It starts to get tight when the tunnel is **17cm** high. Then it gets **7 tenths** lower, then an extra **1 hundredth** lower, then an extra **8 thousandths** lower.

Work out the height of the tunnel: **17 − 7 tenths − 1 hundredth − 8 thousandths**. Can you fit?

Turn over and check your answers on page 94. Add **1 point** to your full speed. Then you can either complete the extra exercise on page 94 or carry on with the story on page 95.

1] a) 0.05   **b)** $\dfrac{9}{1000}$ **c) 4**

2] a) 14.742+1.544 = **16.286cm**   **b)** 56.723 + 1.893 = **58.616cm**

3] The tunnel is **16.282cm** high (17 - 0.7 - 0.01 - 0.008). So no, you can't fit.

EXTRA EXERCISE

First, cover the answer at the bottom of the page! The tunnel also gets narrower as well as lower. It is **59.590cm** wide. Then it gets **8 tenths** narrower, then an extra **9 hundredths** narrower, then an extra **5 thousandths** narrower.

How narrow does the tunnel get? Check your answer and add **1 point** to your full strength. Now carry on with the story on page 95.

EXTRA EXERCISE: Answers

59.590 – 0.8 – 0.09 – 0.005 = **58.695cm** wide (so you actually could have fitted width-wise. Never mind).

"I can't fit, we'll have to clear it," you call back to Gord, beginning to shuffle backwards out of the hole.

"What?"

"I can't fit! It's too tight!"

And then, as you shift your weight, your elbow sinks into the ground. You hear a crack spidering out beneath you.

Oh no...

"Gord, grab my feet!" you yell, but it's too late. The ground you're lying on gives way and you fall right through it.

CHAPTER TWELVE:
What Are You Doing Here?

For a few seconds you are weightless in the darkness. *This is going to hurt*, you think.

But then you land, and thankfully it's with an almighty *splash* rather than an almighty *splat*. Water. It takes you by surprise, and you inhale a mouthful of it and choke in the depths, your lungs and chest aching.

With effort you swim to the surface and spit, gasping for air. "*Oh God...*" you splutter, frantically treading water as your armour tries to drag you down.

Then your eyes adjust to the gloom.

You are in a huge cavern, with lit torches lining the walls. You've landed in the underground river. With effort you make it to the riverbank, which is cold black stone, and haul yourself out.

"*Aquaan!*" You hear Gord's voice high above you.

"I'm okay!" you shout back, and then cough out more water. "I've found the river!"

"The blockage has shifted quite a lot! I can see a way through!"

"Wait there! And be careful you don't fall through the floor like I did! I'm going to find a way up to you!"

Luckily, your weapon has fallen on the stone floor rather than in the river, so you pick it up and stand straight, dripping wet. With a little concentration your magic seeps into the water soaking you, and you lift it free from your skin and clothes and fling it across the stone. You are instantly dry again.

"What is this place..." you mutter to yourself, looking round in wonder.

The vast cavern is natural rather than man-made, but it has been decorated with a dozen large serpentine statues around the walls. The torches cast flickering shadows, making it look like they're moving.

Maybe Al'Nor just really likes snakes, you think, but you are uneasy. And as you approach one of the statues for a closer look you feel your skin prickle.

They're not snakes.

They look like snakes at first glance, but the heads are flatter, with long pointy ears, and they have six small, crab-like legs low on their tubular bodies.

They are *Dakree*.

Monsters, from deep within Numera's crust.

Those from Below.

"How..." you mumble. "Why would..."

And then you notice the bones, strewn about in the darkness. Human. And they have fang marks on them.

Al'Nor has been feeding people to the Dakree.

You take in the breadth of the cavern again, now your eyes have adjusted. The river cuts through the middle. There are metal grills at either end, allowing the river rush through, but the bars are not wide enough for you.

Guess I can't just swim under, then. So how to get out of here?

You can see one huge stone door, with engravings of that serpentine Dakree creature. That'd be a good start. You start to head towards it when...

"H-hello?"

The voice startles you, and you spin round, raising your weapon. For a moment you see nothing, then the man's fallen shape materialises out of the darkness. He lies on his back, motionless, apart from the rise and fall of his chest.

"Who are you?" you ask, standing over him.

"I'm Two Fifteen," he manages.

"Just after lunch."

"What?"

"Nothing. What are you doing here?"

"I cut my arm in The Pit... it's p-pretty bad." He's pressing his left hand to his right bicep, trying to stem the bleeding. "I guess I'm useless." He is weak and pale from blood loss.

"What were you doing in The Pit? What's going on down there?"

He shakes his head and says, "Just... digging. We're digging. I don't know why, or what for. Al'Nor just keeps yelling, *'Deeper!'* at us, and hitting us with his stick." He coughs meekly. "Hey, you need to get out of here. There are... *things* down here..."

"Things?"

"They're monsters, I tell you. I ain't never seen the like before. Scuttling around like massive crab things."

Aoulömm, you think, pronounced *Ow-lom*, which is the Dakree word for *crab-spider*. *Massive crab things* is not a bad description.

"What about monsters that look like snakes?" you ask.

Two Fifteen shakes his head. "You've seen the statues? I don't know what those things are, but no. These giant crabs are different. I guess when they're hungry they'll... they'll..."

You purse your lips. "If it makes you feel any better, you'll be dead in ten minutes, I reckon. From the blood loss."

He actually chuckles. "Thanks."

You have a choice. You can tear off a strip from the guy's shirt as a bandage, using one of your precious goatweed poultices or finberry roots to try and save his life. It might be too late, but you can try.

Or you can save your medical supplies for your own needs and leave him die. Decide now.

If you decide to try and save him, cross off a goatweed or finberry root from your items. Your reputation goes up by 1 point. If you let him die, you keep your supplies, but your reputation goes down by 1 point. Do the necessary adjustments.

At that moment you hear scuttling.

"Oh no..." Two Fifteen gasps. "Run... *hide!*"

"I don't think so." You watch them come, out of the walls. They *are* aoulömm. Crab-spiders. They move slowly at first, sizing you up.

"Hi," you say, "it's been a while. I forget - can you things speak?"

They start running towards you, their jaws clicking excitedly. No, they can't speak.

Two Fifteen screams. But you are an Elemental. You have water magic... and a river right at your feet.

Remember, to activate your magic you need to complete this challenge. And it's pretty important you do. Remember to cover the answers with your scrap piece of paper. Half of these questions are division, so you can have **two minutes**. If you get 16 or more, you activate your magic. If you don't, I'm afraid these crab-spiders from Below will kill you. So you should retake the test until you've managed it.

THE TEST				
1) 8x8=	**2)** 4x6=	**3)** 3x6=	**4)** 7x2=	**5)** 11x12=
6) 4x5=	**7)** 9x3=	**8)** 6x7=	**9)** 4x8=	**10)** 7x9=
11) 30÷5=	**12)** 32÷4=	**13)** 56÷8=	**14)** 121÷11=	**15)** 16÷2=
16) 63÷9=	**17)** 49÷7=	**18)** 24÷3=	**19)** 18÷6=	**20)** 84÷7=

ANSWERS						
1) 64	2) 24	3) 18	4) 14	5) 132	6) 20	7) 27
8) 42	9) 32	10) 63	11) 6	12) 8	13) 7	14) 11
15) 8	16) 7	17) 7	18) 8	19) 3	20) 12	

There are six of the horrible critters, and they attack in two separate groups.

Group 1 consists of the four crab-spiders you see to the right and below. Group 2 consists of the remaining two crab-spiders which haven't reached you yet.

Cast one spell on the first group now. Arrow Rain, okay? And remember the water source is the *river*. You don't have to cross anything off your items (assuming you have anything to cross off).

Then finish off the Group One crab-spiders as normal. For the first time, your enemies may be faster than you. If your speed is 12 or lower, the crab-spider on the right attacks you first. *Then you can attack.* And then the four crab-spiders attack you in turn before you get your go again. You know how this works.

If you fall, return to checkpoint 5 on page 93.

Group One Crab-spider

Stre 19	Spd 12

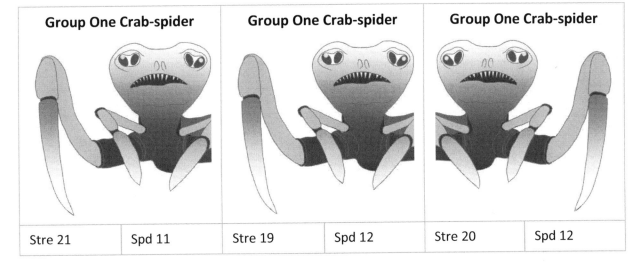

Group One Crab-spider		**Group One Crab-spider**		**Group One Crab-spider**	
Stre 21	Spd 11	Stre 19	Spd 12	Stre 20	Spd 12

The last two crab-spiders have reached you and there isn't time to cast a spell. You need to fight them hand-to-hand. Or hand-to-clickety-clackety-claw, in this case. Again, if your speed is 12 or lower then you don't go first. You may need to use a finberry root or goatweed poultice. If you fall, return to checkpoint 5 on page 93.

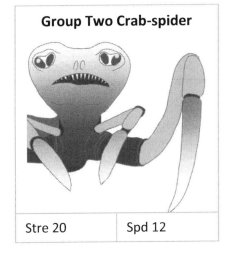

Group Two Crab-spider

Stre 20	Spd 12

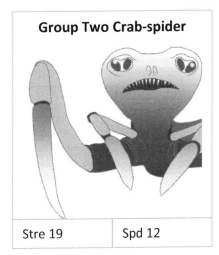

Group Two Crab-spider

Stre 19	Spd 12

The monsters lie strewn across the cavern floor like skittles. You can still feel the mist on your skin, the remnants of the spell, and the adrenaline looping up and down your body.

Dakree here? In a gold mine, in the God-forsaken mountains of Sha'Pan?

"What are you doing here..." you mutter to yourself.

You turn to see if Two Fifteen has the answer, or will at least praise your delightful magical abilities, but Two Fifteen is dead.

You sigh. If you've wasted one of your precious healing plants on him, you sigh twice, but at least you know you did all you could.

The cracks in the walls the crab-spiders crawled out of are too tight for you, so you turn your attention back to the huge stone door, with the snake-like Dakree engravings. That looks like your only way out of here.

Next to the door is a lever, with a chain connected to what seems to be an elaborate pulley system set into the wall. But when you pull the lever the chain simply goes slack, and you notice the counterweight on the other side is far too light. There are pieces of stone scattered across the floor, and you realise that you can use these pieces as weights.

Checkpoint 6
Worksheet Topic 11
FRACTIONS

EQUIVALENT FRACTIONS

Equivalent means *'the same'* or *'equal'*. Imagine a pizza. Yummy. Now cut the pizza in half (pic 1) and then in half again, into quarters (pic 2). As you can see, eating **1 half** a pizza is the same as eating **2 quarters** of pizza.

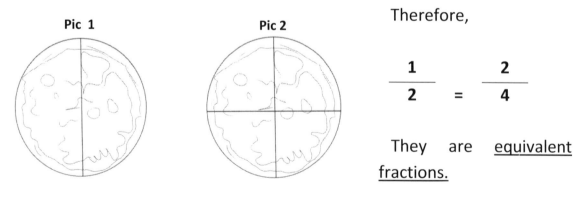

Therefore,

$$\frac{1}{2} = \frac{2}{4}$$

They are <u>equivalent fractions.</u>

You can calculate equivalent fractions by multiplying or dividing **both** the numerator and denominator by the **same** number.

For instance, let's say we want to calculate equivalent fractions of ½. If we multiply both the numerator and denominator by 2 we get two quarters, as above. If we multiply them by **3** or **4** or **5**...

1] Calculate the following equivalent fractions of ½.

a) $\dfrac{1 \quad \text{x3} =}{2 \quad \text{x3} =}$ ____

b) $\dfrac{1 \quad \text{x4} =}{2 \quad \text{x4} =}$ ____

c) $\dfrac{1 \quad \text{x5} =}{2 \quad \text{x5} =}$ ____

2] Complete the following equivalent fractions, filling in the shaded areas.

a) $\dfrac{2 \quad \text{x2} =}{5 \quad \text{x2} =}$ ____

b) $\dfrac{9 \quad \div 3 =}{24 \quad \div 3 =}$ ____

c) $\dfrac{15}{25} \quad = \quad \dfrac{3}{5}$

d) $\dfrac{\quad \text{x4} =}{\quad \text{x4} =} \dfrac{12}{28}$

e) $\dfrac{\quad \div 6 = \quad 6}{66 \quad \div 6 =}$

f) $\dfrac{5}{6} \quad \overset{=}{=} \quad \dfrac{35}{\ }$

Check your answers on page 103 and add **1 point** to your full speed.

ORDERING FRACTIONS

To order fractions from smallest to largest, the denominators must be the same. If they're <u>not</u> the same, you need to <u>make them</u> the same by finding equivalent fractions. Then you can simply compare the numerators.

1] Order the following fractions from smallest to largest: $\dfrac{9}{15}$, $\dfrac{5}{15}$, $\dfrac{6}{15}$

2] Order the following fractions from smallest to largest. You will first have to decide on the *common denominator*.

$$\dfrac{12}{16} , \dfrac{3}{12} , \dfrac{4}{8}$$

Check your answers on page 103 and add **1 point** to your full strength.

An **improper fraction** is where the numerator is **bigger** than the denominator. Something like six quarters (6 over 4), for instance. You can change improper fractions into **mixed numbers**. A mixed number is a mix of whole numbers and fractions, like 2⅖ or similar.

$$\frac{12}{7} \quad \text{Is the same as} \quad 1\frac{5}{7}$$

We start with **12 sevenths**. *7 sevenths* make a *whole*. So we have **one whole** and *5 sevenths* left over (because 12-7 =5).

First, cover page 103! It has the answers on it.

1] Write the following improper fractions as mixed numbers.

a) $\dfrac{6}{4}$

b) $\dfrac{12}{5}$

c) $\dfrac{17}{9}$

Check your answers on page 103. Add **1 point** to *either* your full strength or full speed. You choose. Then fully replenish your attributes. If you wish, you can complete the extra exercises below. Else continue with the story on page 104.

EXTRA EXERCISE

1] Look at the following fractions / mixed numbers.

$$\frac{7}{12} \qquad 2\frac{3}{4} \qquad \frac{5}{6} \qquad \frac{7}{3} \qquad \frac{16}{24}$$

Put them in order from smallest to largest. First find a common denominator using equivalent fractions (HINT: Think of your **multiples** here, rather than common factors. The denominator you need is bigger than you may imagine). Then change the mixed number to an improper fraction. Then you can put them in order. Then back to how they looked originally, in the question. Easy!

Then check your answers on page 103. Add **1 point** to both your full speed and full strength Now go to page 104 and continue with the story.

EQUIVALENT FRACTIONS: Answers

1] $\dfrac{1}{2}$ $\begin{array}{l}\times 3 = \\ \times 3 =\end{array}$ $\dfrac{3}{6}$ $\dfrac{1}{2}$ $\begin{array}{l}\times 4 = \\ \times 4 =\end{array}$ $\dfrac{4}{8}$ $\dfrac{1}{2}$ $\begin{array}{l}\times 5 = \\ \times 5 =\end{array}$ $\dfrac{5}{10}$

2] $\dfrac{2}{5}$ $\begin{array}{l}\times 2 = \\ \times 2 =\end{array}$ $\dfrac{4}{10}$ $\dfrac{9}{24}$ $\begin{array}{l}\div 3 = \\ \div 3 =\end{array}$ $\dfrac{3}{8}$ $\dfrac{15}{25}$ $\begin{array}{l}\div 5 = \\ \div 5 =\end{array}$ $\dfrac{3}{5}$

$\dfrac{3}{7}$ $\begin{array}{l}\times 4 = \\ \times 4 =\end{array}$ $\dfrac{12}{28}$ $\dfrac{36}{66}$ $\begin{array}{l}\div 6 = \\ \div 6 =\end{array}$ $\dfrac{6}{11}$ $\dfrac{5}{6}$ $\begin{array}{l}\times 7 = \\ \times 7 =\end{array}$ $\dfrac{35}{42}$

ORDERING FRACTIONS: Answers

1] $\dfrac{5}{15}$, $\dfrac{6}{15}$, $\dfrac{9}{15}$

2] $\dfrac{12}{16}$, $\dfrac{3}{12}$, $\dfrac{4}{8}$ Make equivalent: $\dfrac{3}{4}$, $\dfrac{1}{4}$, $\dfrac{2}{4}$

In order: $\dfrac{1}{4}$, $\dfrac{2}{4}$, $\dfrac{3}{4}$ In original format: $\dfrac{3}{12}$, $\dfrac{4}{8}$, $\dfrac{12}{16}$

IMPROPER FRACTIONS & MIXED NUMBERS: Answers

a) $\dfrac{6}{4} = 1\dfrac{2}{4}$ b) $\dfrac{12}{5} = 2\dfrac{2}{5}$ c) $\dfrac{17}{9} = 1\dfrac{8}{9}$

EXTRA EXERCISE: Answers

STEP 1: $\dfrac{7}{12}$ $2\dfrac{9}{12}$ $\dfrac{10}{12}$ $\dfrac{28}{12}$ $\dfrac{8}{12}$

STEP 2: $\dfrac{7}{12}$ $\dfrac{33}{12}$ $\dfrac{10}{12}$ $\dfrac{28}{12}$ $\dfrac{8}{12}$

STEP 3: $\dfrac{7}{12}$ $\dfrac{16}{24}$ $\dfrac{5}{6}$ $\dfrac{7}{3}$ $2\dfrac{3}{4}$

You order and sort the fractions of rock, smallest to largest, and slot them into their places on the counterweight. Then you try the lever again. This time, the chain pulls taut and the pulley pulls and the counterweight rises, and so does the door.

You find yourself in a wide tunnel, the river rushing along beside you on your right, lit torches lining the wall on your left. That cold sinking feeling hasn't left your stomach. What are the Dakree doing here? Why have they settled in an old gold mine in the middle of the Sha'Pan mountains? *What's their plan?*

Wary you are, but with the river running next to you, the source for your magic, you also feel more powerful than you've felt since your fight with Drojinn the flying snake monster.

There are more bones here, along the walls. And then you hear scuttling from further up the path, and the clicking jaws of those crab-spiders.

More of them.

And amid the high pitched clickety-clicks there's a lower, slower *clack-clack.* You can tell it's from a larger and stronger beast. And then you see them. They emerge from the gloom, scuttling towards you, two regular sized crab-spiders and one crab-spider queen, more than twice the size of the other two.

You need to activate your magic. You know what that means. Cover the answers at the bottom of the page with your scrap paper. You have **2 minutes**. You need 16 correct, else retake the test.

If your speed is the greater, remember you can also attack one of the enemies after you've cast your magic – casting a spell does **not** count as your 'turn'. I'd suggest focusing on the queen. She ain't no gentle lady.

If you fall in the following battle, return to checkpoint 6 on page 100.

THE TEST				
1)4x8=	2)4x6=	3)11x10=	4)9x2=	5)12x12=
6)6x5=	7)9x9=	8)6x8=	9)3x8=	10)7x6=
11)55÷5=	12)12÷4=	13)48÷8=	14)132÷11=	15)14÷2=
16)36÷9=	17)21÷7=	18)18÷3=	19)30÷6=	20)84÷7=

ANSWERS						
1) 32	2) 24	3) 110	4) 18	5) 144	6) 30	7) 81
8) 48	9) 24	10) 42	11) 11	12) 3	13) 6	14) 12
15) 7	16) 4	17) 3	18) 6	19) 5	20) 12	

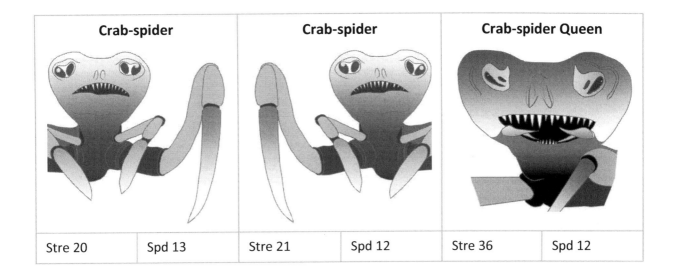

Crab-spider		Crab-spider		Crab-spider Queen	
Stre 20	Spd 13	Stre 21	Spd 12	Stre 36	Spd 12

The queen collapses amid the scattered remains of the two smaller crab-spiders and gives off a foul stench like an open sewer. You stretch your back, breathing deeply, and say, "Crab pâté, anyone?"

No one wants no crab pâté.

You heal yourself with the river (so go on and completely replenish your attributes) and then continue walking.

Eventually you reach the end of the tunnel. The river rushes through a grill in the wall. There's an iron gate like a portcullis on the path, and you can see the next room through it, which is circular, with the river cutting through it like a frothy silver scar.

There's a keyhole in the gate and a lockbox screwed to the wall. Someone has scratched an equation onto the rock. Perhaps it was one of the crab-spiders. Ha.

Checkpoint 7

Worksheet Topic 12
ADDING, SUBTRACTING & MULTIPLYING FRACTIONS

Adding and subtracting fractions is easy peasy **when the denominators are the same**. If the denominators are different, you need to make them the same by using your equivalent fractions knowledge and finding a common denominator.

When the denominators are the same, you simply **add or subtract the numerators only**. You don't have to do anything to the denominator.

eg.) $$\frac{3}{8} - \frac{1}{8} + \frac{2}{8} = \frac{3-1+2}{8} = \frac{4}{8}$$

Now cover the answers on page 107!

1] Answer the following. You will first need to find the common denominators.

a) $\frac{1}{2} + \frac{2}{6} - \frac{1}{3} =$ **b)** $\frac{3}{4} - \frac{1}{3} + \frac{3}{12} =$ **c)** $\frac{6}{7} - \frac{3}{4} + \frac{1}{2} =$

2] Solve this equation. Give your answer as a <u>mixed number</u>.

$$2\frac{3}{4} - 1\frac{2}{5} =$$

HINT: A good way to find a common denominator is to simply multiply the denominators together. Then you know both denominators must be factors.

Multiplying with fractions isn't hugely difficult. You multiply by the numerator and divide by the denominator. And do whichever is easier <u>first</u>. Also, a fraction **of** a number means multiply.

To solve $\frac{3}{4}$ of **8** $8 \times 3 = 24$, and then $24 \div 4 = 6$

         OR $8 \div 4 = 2$, and then $2 \times 3 = 6$.

If you are multiplying by a mixed number, multiply the fraction part as above, then multiply the whole number, and then add the two answers.

eg.) What is $2\frac{2}{3} \times 3$

First multiply the fraction: $3 \times 2 = 6$, and then $6 \div 3 = $ **2**.

Then the whole number: $2 \times 3 = $ **6**.

Add them together: $2 + 6 = $ **8**

3] What is $\dfrac{2}{5}$ of **15**

4] What is $3\dfrac{2}{3} \times 9$

Check your answers below and add **1 point** to your full strength or full speed. Now either continue with the story on page 108 or complete the extra exercise.

Now either continue with the story on page 108 or complete the extra exercise.

EXTRA EXERCISE

Solve $\left(2\dfrac{3}{4} \times 8\right) + \dfrac{2}{3} - \dfrac{1}{2} =$

First do the multiplication, then add on the two thirds, then take off the half. Check your answer below and add **1 point** to your full strength or full speed. Now continue with the story on page 108.

Now continue with the story on page 108.

ADDING, SUBTRACTING & MULTIPLYING FRACTIONS: Answers

1] Answer the following. You will first need to find the common denominators.

a) $\dfrac{3}{6}$ **b)** $\dfrac{8}{12}$ **c)** $\dfrac{17}{28}$

2] Solve this equation. Give your answer as a <u>mixed number</u>.

$$2\dfrac{15}{20} - 1\dfrac{8}{20} = 1\dfrac{7}{20}$$

3] 6 **4]** 33

EXTRA EXERCISE: Answer

$22\dfrac{1}{6}$

The lockbox pops wide, and you take the key and unlock the gate. It squeaks as you push it open and enter the circular room. There's a hole in the ceiling with a rope hanging through it, and a bucket on the end of the rope. You've found the well, albeit from below. Not exactly what you had in mind. There's a metal door in the wall, but it's locked. No worries.

First thing's first: you have three empty water skins. You fill them up with river water, so you can use them as a water source for what's to come.

Add them to your items now.

You sheathe your weapon, then you jump and grab hold of the bucket. You worry that the rope will unravel and dump you into the river, but it holds your weight.

You start to climb.

CHAPTER THIRTEEN:
Out Of The Well

You swing gently on the rope as you ascend, hand-over-hand. You can hear the murmur of voices above. Eventually the well's stone circular wall surrounds you, and you brace your feet against it and reach out your hands, one-by-one, taking hold of the lip.

"What are we even digging for?" someone says. "There's nothing down there."

"He must have a reason."

"I'm not sure he does, to be honest. I don't think he knows what's going on anymore. Do you think he's... losing it?"

"Losing it?"

"Yes. I'm being serious. You must have noticed. He's been acting so weird these last few months. What's this obsession with The Pit? He literally lives on a gold mine, and yet he keeps pulling the strongest prisoners we got out of it. Putting them in this hole which, from what I can gather, *is just dirt*."

"It's not our job to question him, Lieutenant, it's to protect him."

Lieutenant? These were a couple of Al'Nor's personal bodyguard, then.

"I know," said the other, "but there's something really up with him. And then we have one of the Eleven show up..."

"You don't know it's one of the Eleven."

"Well the guards keep saying the same thing, don't they – *magic* – so it sounds like it to me."

You slowly lift your eyes above the lip of the well. The two men have their backs to you. They're huddled over a table, on which there is a candlestick and rolls of parchment.

You silently rise up out of the well and sit on the wall, watching them argue.

"Magic? Bah. I don't believe it. Not unless I see it with my own eyes."

The Lieutenant looks at the floor. "That's not all, though, is it? There are *things* down there..."

"Things?"

"Come on, you've heard them. You've heard what happens to the people sent down there. Down to the river." And he turns and looks at the well, and finds you sitting atop it, with your weapon lying across your knees, listening.

You say, "Don't stop on my account. I want to hear more about Al'Nor's impending senility."

They exchange shocked glances.

"*Senility,*" you say again. "Going senile? You said that Al'Nor... oh, never mind."

One of the bodyguards grabs his sword and growls, "Where the hell did you come from?"

"Out of the well..." says the other.

You nod. "Correct. And I can confirm that there definitely are *things* down there. So I don't know what your master has been playing at but I think you better start talking, don't you?"

Instead of talking, the bodyguards run at you. It's not exactly a sneak attack, so they don't get to attack you first, but you don't have time to faff around with your magic either.

You'll have to defeat these guys hand-to-hand. But there's only two of them.

If your speed is 15 or less, the bodyguard on the left attacks you first. Then your go. If you fall, checkpoint 7 is on page 105. One of the bodyguards drops a finberry root. Add it to your items if you have room (you can only carry 3 medical supplies).

Bodyguard

| Stre 20 | Spd 15 |

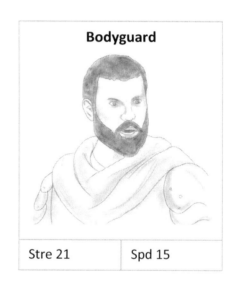

Bodyguard

| Stre 21 | Spd 15 |

The chairs have been thrown aside in the melee. One is broken, and has a bodyguard lodged in it. The other bodyguard lies against the well.

You make your way up to the table and inspect the parchment. There are two letters. Handwritten.

One says in an elegant script:

> Send all the men to the pit. All of them. If it really <u>is</u> one of the Eleven, then we'll need everyone.
>
> We are so close now. Failure is not an option.

It is signed *Al'Nor.*

The second letter startles you.

We have heard news from the rangers. They have received word that a strange traveller has been asking questions about us. And more specifically about one of the prisoners. The traveller is described as a bald man in a white robe, and he has the tattoo of an eye on the back of one hand. These reports are a week old, but be wary, just in case.

You feel your heart pick up speed, because you know the man described in the letter. Psi. Another one of the Eleven. Powerful psychic abilities. He's trying to rescue you. Except it says the reports are a week old already. And you have no idea when the letter was written. Could have been a month ago.

So where is he? What's happened to him?

When you lost your staff you lost all ways of contacting the others, and they could no longer contact you. Until you get it back you're on your own. But that's okay; you're doing pretty well, wouldn't you say?

There is a larger sheet of parchment, and this one will come in handy. It is a map of Sha'Pan, showing the gold mine and surrounding landmarks, roads, and settlements. You roll it up and take it with you.

According to the first letter you read, Al'Nor has had all his troops brought down The Pit. But why? To protect him? To protect whatever they're trying to achieve?

You think of the Lieutenant's words. *"What are we even digging for? There's nothing down there."* Well, Al'Nor obviously thinks there is.

Outside, the corridor is deserted. You head towards the food store, which your original map of the mine shows you is right round the next corner. The door is unguarded, but like so many doors in this place, it is locked with a complicated mechanism.

Worksheet Topic 13
DECIMALS

You have already done some work on decimals earlier in the book – adding with them, multiplying by multiples of 10 etc. You can also write fractions as decimals, and decimals as fractions.

0.1 is the same as **one tenth**: $\frac{1}{10}$

0.01 is the same as **one hundredth**: $\frac{1}{100}$

0.001 is the same as **one thousandth**: $\frac{1}{1000}$

Now cover the answers at the bottom of the page.

1] Write the following decimals as fractions (or mixed numbers if required).

a) 0.02   **b)** 2.3   **c)** 0.463   **d)** 3.002   **e)** 0.2

Rounding decimals is exactly the same process as rounding whole numbers, but instead of rounding to the nearest hundred, or thousand, or whatever, you will be rounding to one decimal place, or two decimal places etc.

  One decimal place means there is **one** number after the decimal point. So you would look at the number to the right of that and use it as the decider.

eg.) Round **0.046** to <u>two</u> decimal places.

The second decimal place is the 4 hundredths. So the 6 thousandths is the decider. You round up if the decider is 5 or above, so 0.046 is rounded to **0.05** to two decimal places.

2] Round **3.533** to <u>one</u> decimal place.

3] Round **0.7095** to <u>three</u> decimal places.

4] Which number is bigger, **0.402, 0.042** or **0.42**?

Now check your answers below, and add **1 point** to either your full speed or full strength. You choose.

DECIMALS: Answers

1] a) 0.02 = $\dfrac{2}{100}$ **b)** 2.3 = $2\dfrac{3}{10}$ **c)** 0.463 = $\dfrac{463}{1000}$ **d)** 3.002 = $3\dfrac{2}{1000}$ **e)** 0.2 = $\dfrac{2}{10}$

2] 3.5

3] 0.710

4] First step: **0.402, 0.042, 0.420.** Then arrange by place value: **0.042, 0.402, 0.420.** So **0.42** is the largest number.

The locking mechanism consists of three dials, with numbers round the outside and a decimal point acting as a pointer on the dial itself. By completing the previous exercises you manage to spring the mechanism and the door clicks open.

The food store is well stocked.

If you wish you can eat the best of the food now, and forget about the needs of the other hungry prisoners. If you do, your full strength increases by +2... but your reputation decreases by 1. Decide if you're going to eat now or not.

Okay. Time to get the others.

This is the plan: the prisoners make it here, collect their supplies and then leave the mine via the main gate.

You will not leave with them. You want your staff back, and you know Al'Nor has it. That little stable child told you so.

You analyse the map of the gold mine once more, reassure yourself of the way, and follow the corridor. You expect enemies to jump out at you at every turn, but all you find is empty passageways. You're aware that beneath you lies that vast cavern, and the river, and those crab-spider things. The Dakree.

Hopefully the floor won't collapse again.

Finally you reach the cave-in, this time from the other side. Gord and the other prisoners have cleared most of it. They've hung around waiting for you to reappear.

Gord lets out a sigh of relief. "Oh, thank God. You're okay."

"Just about," you say. "Any problems?"

"No. You?"

"No." You decide not to tell them about the monsters running around below their feet. "I'm going to take you to the well and to the food store. Take what you need, then get out of here, okay? All of you. Take the horses and go."

You help them climb over the rubble, avoiding the hole in the floor and the dark Dakree cavern far below.

You can hear the river rushing down in the darkness. Every now and then you think you hear a *clickety-click* as well, but it must surely be your imagination.

"This way." You lead them to the food store, and the former prisoners eat their fill and take supplies for the journey. There is more than enough to go around. Then you take them to the well so they can drink and fill their water skins.

"The nearest settlement is less than a day's ride," you say. "Or perhaps two or three days' walk." You unfurl the map of Sha'Pan and point out the landmarks and the road. "Gord, look for these mountains. The road you want runs between them. And then you need to head East at the second fork, with that valley on your left..."

"What are you going to do?"

"Al'Nor has my staff, and I want it back."

"You know, we could do with taking that map."

The others mumble in agreement.

You pause. "The map?"

"That map of Sha'Pan, showing the way to go."

You stare at him. It hadn't occurred to you that they'd want the map. Has taken you a bit off guard, to be honest.

Gord adds, "We'll get lost out there, Aquaan. You know we will."

So what are you going to do?

If you decide to give them the map, go to page 115.

If you decide to keep it for yourself, carry on reading.

You shake your head. "Sorry. I need it."

"What?" He laughs, as if you're joking. "Why do *you* need it? You're an Elemental..."

"Exactly. I don't want to get lost in the mountains either; Numera needs me."

"Oh, right. Needs you more than it needs us, you mean."

You shrug. "Well, yeah."

For some reason they all look appalled at what you think is a pretty obvious fact.

"Look," you say, "when I've got my staff back, I'm going to contact The Eleven. Tell them what's happened, and where I am. *I need to know where I am* so they can find me, and so I can find them."

"Okay, but..."

"I can't let you take it, I'm sorry. *Look at the map*. Remember it. I'm telling you where you need to go, it's not difficult."

"Aquaan, please..."

"*No.*" You shake your head at him, at all of them. "I've set you free. Isn't that enough? What more do you *want?*"

No one says anything for a moment. Then Gord says, "And if we get lost? And we all die? What then?"

You shrug. "I'm sorry, I am. But I don't know why you keep expecting me to be some kind of hero. I'm not."

"No. Obviously." He turns to the others. "Come on. Let's go."

They look at you, full of disappointment, and disdain, and they turn their backs on you and leave.

"I set you free..." you mutter, but no one listens.

You lose 3 reputation points.

Go to page 116.

"You're right," you say, and sigh. "Take it." You hand over the map, and your reputation goes up 2 points.

Then Lilleth says, "Why don't you copy it?"

That's a good idea.

You find a pot of ink in one of the drawers in the table. Better than the bodyguards' blood, anyway.

There's no quill, but you just dip your finger and make a rough copy on the back of one of the letters.

It's *very* rough. And splodgy in places, but it will do.

"Well you wouldn't have made it as a mapmaker," Gord laughs.

"That's okay, it was never a dream of mine." You say, "Time to go."

The group of prisoners you freed stares at you. Feet shuffle.

For a long moment no one knows what to say.

Then Gord takes your hand. "Thank you. My friend."

You nod. "Safe travels."

"And to you."

Go to page 116.

You watch them go, and then you sigh.

Okay. Where now.

You look at the map of the mines and find the way to Al'Nor's rooms. You have to go past the barracks to get to them, but there's literally no one about. When Al'Nor summoned everyone he *meant* everyone.

You reach a staircase, and suddenly everything seems lighter and brighter. The heaviness from the mines lifts. You can't taste dust anymore. The staircase is hewed out of the stone, but you can see windows further up – *actual windows* looking out on the *actual sky*.

You put away the map and head on up, as the stairs spiral up the tower. It is still raining outside. You pass the first window, and then the second, and through the third you can see the mountains in the distance, and the sun beginning to set.

You finally reach the top. The door to Al'Nor's residence is ajar. You slip inside, as quiet as a shadow. There are silk drapes hanging from the ceiling, and billowing against the breeze from the open balcony doors. The floor is polished marble.

There are statues and paintings. All of him. Al'Nor. A younger, better-looking, more toned version of him.

And in one corner, next to the four-poster bed, is a large wooden chest with about five padlocks on it. You kneel down next to it and examine one of them. "Okay," you say, and let out a breath. You think of your staff. The average person wouldn't understand, but your staff is like a part of you. "Please be in here."

Checkpoint 8

Worksheet Topic 14
PERCENTAGES

'Per Cent' means *'out of a hundred'*. So 50% (fifty percent) simply means 50 out of 100. Which is **half**. This is because: $\frac{50}{100}_{(\div 10)} = \frac{5}{10}_{(\div 5)} = \frac{1}{2}$

Converting percentages to decimals is *easy peasy*.

100% = 1   **80% = 0.8**   **66% = 0.66**   **25% = 0.25**   **10% = 0.1**

Converting percentages to fractions isn't too hard either.

100% = $\frac{100}{100}$ **80% = $\frac{80}{100}$**   **66% = $\frac{66}{100}$**   **25% = $\frac{25}{100}$**   **10% = $\frac{10}{100}$**

First, cover the answers at the bottom of the page!

1] Write the following percentages as both decimals and fractions.

a) 20%   **b) 16%**   **c) 99%**   **d) 75%**

2] Convert these decimals and fractions into percentages.

a) 0.7   **b) 0.02**   **c)** $\dfrac{3}{4}$ **d)** $\dfrac{1}{5}$ **e)** $\dfrac{9}{10}$

3] What is 60% of 300?   (HINT: make the percentage a fraction)

Check your answers below. Add **1 point** to <u>both</u> your full strength and full speed, then replenish your attributes. Then either complete the extra exercise below or continue with the story on page 118.

EXTRA EXERCISE

1] Imagine there are 25 enemies, and you have defeated 17 of them. What percentage of the total enemies have you defeated?

HINT: write as a fraction. Now what does the denominator need to be for a percentage?

Check your answer below. Add **1 point** to either your full strength or full speed. Then continue with the story on page 118.

PERCENTAGES: Answers

1] a) 20% = 0.2 = $\dfrac{20}{100}$ **b)** 16% = 0.16 = $\dfrac{16}{100}$ **c)** 99% = 0.99 = $\dfrac{99}{100}$ **d)** 75% = 0.75 = $\dfrac{75}{100}$

2] a) 70%   **b) 2%**   **c) 75%**   **d) 20%**   **e)**   **90%**

3] 60% of 300 = $\dfrac{60}{100}$ x 300.   300÷100 = 3.   3x60 = **180**.

EXTRA EXERCISE: Answer

1] You have defeated $\dfrac{17}{25}$ enemies. $\dfrac{17}{25}$ = $\dfrac{68}{100}$ = **68%.**
                                              (x4)

The padlocks click and fall off one by one.

You hope to God your staff is in there. But a large, nagging part of you thinks this chest will be empty.

Your heart flutters as you slowly lever open the chest.

It's not empty.

Your staff isn't in there, but the chest is not empty.

Inside you find the body of Al'Nor.

CHAPTER FOURTEEN:
Then Who?

You can tell straight away that he's been dead a while. Probably months.

You slam the chest shut, having had enough of the smell.

Your mind reels. If Al'Nor has been dead for a good while, who was that in the cell block this morning? Because it sure looked and sounded and acted like Al'Nor.

Then you remember the Lieutenant's words, overheard whilst you were climbing out of the well.

You must have noticed. He's been acting so weird these last few months.

Well, it appears the reason Al'Nor has been acting so weird is because he's really dead in a chest in his bedroom. Whoever you saw this morning - whoever has been obsessed with The Pit all this time – is someone *pretending* to be Al'Nor.

Or something. A shapeshifter.

That's when Caesar, Al'Nor's High Protector, walks out from one of the side rooms. He starts a little when he sees you, shocked. He is carrying a bucket of something. Maybe he's just unclogged the toilet. "*You...*"

"Me." You stand up. "Didn't expect to see you here, Caesar."

"It's *sir* to you."

"Okay, Sir Caesar. Caesar the Geezer. Caesar the Fridge Freezer."

"I recognise your face. You were one of our prisoners."

"How about Caesar Salad? Do you like that nickname?"

He notices the padlocks from the chest are on the floor. "You opened it."

"I was looking for my staff."

Caesar frowns, and then realisation dawns across his face. "Oh, that's *your* staff."

"Do you know where it is?"

"The master's got it."

You stare at him. "The master. Do you... know what's in the chest?"

Caesar swallows. He nods. "Yes. I have a new master now."

You circle around the room towards him. He backs up against the wall, then grabs one of the wall torches. It is lit.

"Careful," you say, "you'll set fire to your beard."

Instead, he plunges the lit torch into the bucket. There is a hissing sound, and you wonder for a moment whether he has a bucketful of snakes. But then he throws the contents at you. About a dozen sparking, spitting metal balls.

And then you realise what they are. They're *bombs*. Presumably the thing pretending to be Al'Nor wanted them for The Pit.

Instead, you've got them all to yourself.

You dive away as the metal balls explode, feel the rush of hot, burnt air from the blast, feel it lift you and fling you against the wall like a rag doll. Stone and debris flies this way and that. You can hear stone cracking, and debris raining down, and fire crackling, and a high-pitched ringing that comes from inside your head.

Then a strong wind whips around you, lashing rain against your face, waking you from your stupor. You lift your head. The blast has knocked Caesar off his feet too. He is crawling across the marble like a lizard. Above him, above you both, the silk drapes are burning.

There's a hole in the wall next to you, and the rain whirls about and splashes inside. You climb slowly to your feet. "Your master is not going to be happy about what you've done to his house."

You have been damaged by the bombs. Reduce your strength by 4 and your speed by 3.

Caesar doesn't reply. He pulls himself behind one of the statues, using it as cover.

You take in a deep breath, activating your magic, crafting a vortex from the rain outside, drawing it in.

You have a choice. You can either launch the vortex directly at the statue Caesar is sheltering behind (go to Section A below). Or you can launch it at the ceiling above his head, sending it crashing down onto him (go to Section B below).

Section A

You reach forth your arms, and the vortex spins out, crashing into the statue and reducing it to dust. Caesar gets blasted across the room, though was protected from the brunt of the attack.

Look at his character card at the top of the next page. Reduce his strength by 5 and his speed by 2.

Go to page 121.

Section B

You direct the vortex at the ceiling above Caesar's head, and it collapses on top of him. He manages to shelter beneath the statue, which takes most of the impact, but his legs are badly injured.

Look at his character card at the top of the next page. Reduce his strength by 2 and his speed by 4.

Go to page 121.

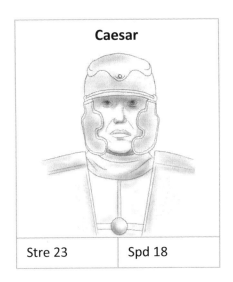

Caesar

Stre 23	Spd 18

Play out the rest of the battle. If you fall, return to checkpoint 8 on page 116.

Caesar staggers to his knees, clutching his side, which is blooming red roses, his sword forgotten. He tries to get back to his feet using the plinth of one of the statues for support, but ends up just lying against it.

"You can't win," he manages. "You're already too late..."

The wind and rain whips around the cracked, burning room. Glowing embers from the flaming drapes float around you like fireflies.

"What's he doing down there?" you ask. "In The Pit?"

Caesar laughs at you. "Digging," he says.

"Digging for *what?*"

The bodyguard stops laughing and grows serious. "That's the wrong question, Aquaan of... wherever you're from. Elemental land. Elemento. Elementallica!"

The floor quakes, and you almost lose your balance.

The bombs have done some serious structural damage. And the fire is growing, and raging. You need to get out of there.

"Then what's the *right* question?" you ask. "*Tell me,* Caesar!"

He grits his teeth, fighting for breath. Then he says, "Don't ask what he's digging *for.* Ask *where* he's digging *to...*"

Another quake. You hear a grinding, tearing, shrieking sound, which doesn't sound good one bit. Then the marble floor cracks in two, and the whole room shifts and lurches downwards.

You scream as you fall, amongst the torrent of dust and fire and smoke and ash. Then everything goes black. It's as if you're floating in the deep dark depths of space. You see nothing. You feel nothing. You hear nothing except a very faint ringing, which sounds like it comes from one of Numera's many moons.

Then everything comes rushing back in like a tidal wave.

121

Blinding light, roaring and crackling and thundering in your ears, and a searing, burning pain all over your body. The world slowly comes back into focus.

You lie on top of one of the battlements amid the rain and a checkerboard of burning rock. Everything feels broken. All the bones in your body. You can't move. You can barely breathe.

The tower has collapsed. There's just a ruin in its place.

As you watch, Caesar appears at the edge, high above you. You must have fallen eight metres to the cold hard rock below.

No wonder it hurt.

Caesar starts laughing hysterically. "I beat you!" he yells. "I won! Now I'm going to finish you!" He starts climbing down the shattered rock face towards you.

Come on, Aquaan. You can't be killed by a man named after a salad. Get up.

With a great effort, you activate your magic. Feel it flow through your body, knitting together your broken bones and other injuries.

Caesar drops down to the battlements, about the length of a tennis court away from you. He pulls a dagger from a sheath on his belt and makes an exhausted kind of victory cry. Then he staggers forward.

You get your limbs working, just about. You turn onto your belly and slither, arm over arm, kicking with your legs, like a marine on an assault course. You reach the castellation wall and haul yourself to your feet. Your legs hold you up, just about.

Caesar lumbers up to you, hacking with the dagger, but you block his wrist with your forearm and strike him in the face. He cries out, striking again, and this time you dodge and grab his arm, grappling him tight.

You wrestle against the battlements, and then you both topple over them, landing on the hard ground and rolling down the slope to the canyon's gaping edge.

Beside you: a deep hundred metre drop to the canyon floor.

You were at the foot of it earlier today.

Caesar is a little way up the slope. He scrabbles for the dagger, which has come to rest just above his left shoulder.

Then turns his attention back to you.

You need your magic. It's the only thing that will save you.

First, cover the answers at the bottom of page 123. Then answer the following questions, which will test everything we've looked at until now.

If you get 11 or less, you must retake it. If you get 12 or 13, go to Section A on page 124. If you get 14 or 15 correct, go to Section B on page 124.

You have **twenty** minutes.

1] Answer the following: **a)** 5 - 9   **b)** -3 + 7   **c)** -2 – 9

2] What is **573 492** to the nearest ten thousand?

3] Which is the biggest number, **35 030,   35 530,   33 503,   35 330**

4] What is 475.8 + 263.8?

5] What is 8345 – 2749?

6] Write down all the factor pairs of 36

7] What is 56.034 x 100?

8] What is 3677 x 26?

9] What is 1783 ÷ 7? (Use a remainder).

10] Write $\dfrac{1}{4}$ as an equivalent fraction.

11] Write the improper fraction $\dfrac{11}{3}$ as a mixed number.

12] What is $\dfrac{1}{2}$ + $\dfrac{2}{3}$? Give your answer as an improper fraction.

13] Answer the following. What is $\dfrac{3}{4}$ of 24?

14] What is 4.2968 to **two** decimal places?

15] What is 40% of 150?

FINAL TEST: Answers

1] a) -4   b) 4   c) -11   **2]** 570 000   **3]** 35 530

4] 739.6   **5]** 5596   **6]** 1x36, 2x18, 3x12, 4x9, 6x6

7] 5603.4   **8]** 95 602   **9]** 254 remainder 5.

10] $\dfrac{2}{8}$ or $\dfrac{3}{12}$ or $\dfrac{4}{16}$ or $\dfrac{5}{20}$ etc.   **11]** **3** $\dfrac{2}{3}$

12] $\dfrac{7}{6}$ **13]** 18   **14]** 4.30   **15]** 60

Section A

You lie on your back as Caesar staggers towards you, lifting the dagger high. And you reach down deep and summon your magic, and the rain glistens and forms a hundred arrow heads in the sky above, and yes, Al'Nor's bodyguard has a dagger, but you have a hundred. And you reach up a hand and bring it down fast and hard, in an exhausted motion, and the arrow rain thrashes down on top of Caesar.

He grimaces as the rain strikes him, crumbling to his knees, and then flat on his face on the cold hard ground.

Go to the *Coda* below.

Section B

You lie on your back as Caesar staggers toward you, lifting the dagger high. And you reach down deep and summon your magic, and the rain warps and spins above your palm.

With one last exhausted motion you fling it in the bodyguard's direction. The frothing vortex launches Caesar far into the air, over the edge and down into the canyon, his scream dying in his throat, until he is lost in the darkness and the rain.

Go to the *Coda* below.

Coda

Shaking, you climb to your feet.

You have no time to rest. That thing pretending to be Al'Nor... you have a horrible feeling you know what it is. And you think you know why it's digging, and what The Pit is for.

Also, it has your staff.

And you want it back.

The adventure continues with *The Pit* (Year 5 Maths Part 2).

Fill in your final attributes here:

Full Strength: . . . .   **Full Speed:** . . . .   **Reputation:** . . . .

Printed in Great Britain
by Amazon